CHRISTIANS IN
THE AFRICAN REVOLUTION

CHRISTIANS
IN THE
AFRICAN REVOLUTION

The Duff Missionary Lectures, 1962

J. W. C. DOUGALL DD

THE SAINT ANDREW PRESS
EDINBURGH

© J. W. C. Dougall DD, 1963

Printed in Great Britain by
William Blackwood & Sons Limited
32 Thistle Street, Edinburgh

TO
J. H. OLDHAM
IN GRATITUDE AND AFFECTION

PREFACE

THE following pages contain an expansion of four lectures delivered in February and March, 1962, in the Chaplaincy Centre of the University of Edinburgh, to an audience consisting partly of students, with a different African chairman on each occasion. In March and April, they were delivered to an audience of churchfolk in the hall of the West Parish Church, Airdrie. Both in Edinburgh and in Airdrie the lectures were followed by an interesting discussion. My thanks are offered to those who made the arrangements and gathered the audiences, particularly to the Rev. J. C. Blackie, B.D., S.T.M., University Chaplain, the Rev. J. A. L. Cheyne, M.A., B.A., Chaplain to Overseas Students, Edinburgh, the Rev. H. C. Donaldson, M.A., Home Organisation Secretary, Foreign Mission Committee, Church of Scotland, the Rev. James Maitland, M.A., West Parish Church, Airdrie, and the Rev. J. B. Cameron, B.D., Flowerhill Church, Airdrie.

I wish to express my thanks also to the Trustees of the Duff Missionary Lectureship for the invitation to deliver the lectures and for the stimulation to fresh thought and study which this provided. The footnotes are to be read as an acknowledgment of much of what I have learnt from others in the course of preparing these lectures.

The burden of the argument in the pages that follow is that the God and Father of our Lord Jesus Christ is behind all life and that all life finds meaning in Him. This conviction is the key to an understanding of the dramatic and often dangerous revolution now proceeding in Africa. African Christians and

7

the friends who come to help them fulfil the missionary calling of the Church when they recognise and respond to God's presence and purpose in that very situation. From this standpoint changes in the missionary pattern are to be expected and welcomed, and terms such as 'home' and 'foreign', 'missionary' and 'national', 'evangelism' and 'service', 'church' and 'mission', 'religious' and 'secular', fall into a strictly subordinate place as particular aspects or activities of, "One Body, One Gospel, One World". The emphasis falls rather on the unity and wholeness of life, the universal scope of the Church's concern with and for the world, and the Lordship of Christ over history as all derived from and necessary to a full understanding of the Christian revelation of the unity of God.

EDINBURGH.
November, 1962.

CONTENTS

I

CHRISTIAN INVOLVEMENT IN AFRICAN EDUCATION

D R. J. H. OLDHAM once remarked to a Government official in Africa: 'All the mistakes in African education have been made by missionaries'. And when this remark had elicited its expected surprise, he added, 'The reason is that they were the only people who could make them since they were the only people engaged in education'.

The first schools in Africa were established by Christian missionaries and for many years they were the only schools. Education, admittedly limited in scope and efficiency, was accepted as an integral part of the missionary enterprise. There was no clear distinction in those days between preaching and teaching. To missionaries imbued with the spirit of the evangelical revival the school was the indispensable means of teaching enquirers and catechumens to read the Gospel story, and education ran parallel with the knowledge of vernacular languages and the beginnings of Bible translation. No doubt there were other motives which influenced the early missionaries. They probably included in their number many who regarded literacy as the best way to open the minds of primitive people. On the whole, however, those who believed that 'men must be polished and refined before they can be enlightened in religious truth' were not to be found in the ranks of the missionaries but among their opponents.[1] Of course the

[1] Hewat, E. G. K.: *Vision and Achievement*. Thos. Nelson & Sons Ltd. 1960. P. I.

education undertaken by missionaries had other aims and other effects. Material improvements and other signs of civilisation accompanied the Gospel. The mission needed buildings and therefore craftsmen. Nearly always the mission had its hospital and dispensary. It needed organisation and finance, so that clerks and book-keepers had to be trained. At the centre, therefore, there would be trade schools and probably the training of hospital assistants and nurses. Yet the evangelical aim which gave primacy to reading was responsible for the vast expansion of little schools of the simplest character which taught little more than the rudiments of reading, writing and arithmetic. The truth of their origin is witnessed by the fact that in many parts of Africa the vernacular equivalent of the English word 'education' is still the infinitive of the verb 'to read', and Christian enquirers were simply 'readers'. There was in all this activity a somewhat naïve assumption—that if the African boy or girl, or more likely the African man (for he was the more likely pupil at that period)—if he learned to read the Gospel, he was well on the way to becoming a Christian, but of the evangelical motive operating in the establishment and expansion of mission schools there can be no question.

In West Africa missionary education, i.e. education provided by missionary agencies, was started early in the nineteenth century. There were mission schools in the Gambia more than a hundred years before Government took any direct responsibility for education.[1] Although Gold Coast (Ghana) and Nigeria had education departments by 1890 and 1903, the mission schools supplied by far the major part of the educational system. In 1920 the Colonial Report for the Gold

[1] Mayhew: *Education in the Colonial Empire*. Longmans, Green & Co. 1938. P. 102.

Coast listed 198 mission schools over against 19 Government schools. Southern Nigeria had 1602 mission schools, only 160 of which received any help from Government, over against 45 Government schools. In East and Central Africa the predominance of missionary effort in education was still more marked. Though Kenya had an education department in 1911, there were still only 5 Government schools in 1920. When I first went out to Africa in 1924 there were no education departments in Uganda, Northern Rhodesia or Nyasaland. Yet Uganda in 1920 had 80,000 pupils in mission schools and Nyasaland had over 2,000 schools,[1] provided by the missions.

These facts of missionary initiative and enterprise in African education are all the more notable when we appreciate the astonishing contrast of the situation as we see it today: 'Education is in fact becoming a central theme in the unfolding processes of modern African history, perhaps indeed the central theme, as it comes to be the chief task and instrument of African government. It is recognised to be the means without which the poverty of Africa cannot be relieved, its resources developed, the health of its people protected, their standard of living raised; without which social transformation will be for the worse and not the better, the political advancement impossible or illusory.' [2]

The truth of these statements will not be contested by those who know Africa most intimately. African people, on the whole, do attach this immense value to education, and for their Governments as for them it is sought for as the means of deliverance from ignorance and backwardness, the indispensable instrument of change, and the best guarantee of future

[1] *Educational Policy in Africa.* Memorandum submitted by the Conference of British Missionary Societies, 1923.
[2] Campbell, J. McLeod: *African History in the Making.* Edinburgh House Press. 1956. Foreword by the Master of Balliol.

political and social progress. Such being the case, we are bound to ask what has happened to the evangelical aim in African education and what part missionary effort and missionary policy have played in bringing about this remarkable change. We take this latter question first.

The most significant changes in outlook took place in the early twenties when the Phelps-Stokes Fund, in co-operation with missionary societies, and with the approval of the British Colonial Office, sent two Commissions to Africa whose reports opened up new possibilities in the relation of education to the needs of the community. They laid the emphasis upon the educational process as the application of knowledge, the practice of habits and the acquisition of skills to improve health, to increase the means of livelihood, particularly through the better use of the land, and to build up a sound home-life in the African villages. The work of these two Phelps-Stokes Commissions, as they were called,[1] might have had only a limited effect but for two other factors. One was the widespread feeling that literary education was unsatisfactory and ineffective, being to all intents and purposes a Western type of education transplanted to Africa with little effort to suit African conditions; the other was that J. H. Oldham, then Secretary of the International Missionary Council, had brought his mind to bear on the question of education as it involved the missionary societies and the Colonial Office and had put before them a deeply considered and comprehensive policy for education in Africa as the common concern of missions and Governments.

This policy of partnership was accepted by the Colonial Office which recognised the help which missions had given

---

[1] *Education in Africa* (1922) and *Education in East Africa* (1924). Edinburgh House Press and Phelps-Stokes Fund.

and could continue to give, all the more so because the objectives of education as now defined in relation to the environment and the community in Africa were such as Colonial administrators could happily endorse. On the other hand, because of their confidence in Oldham's disinterested concern for African education and the breadth of the missionary experience brought together from India as well as from Africa, Government accepted the principle of private or voluntary agencies for education working with State supervision and support. This was approved not only because it rendered possible a far more rapid expansion of education than Government could achieve by its own efforts, but also because it gave the system a flexibility and variety which was the best safeguard against a rigid and bureaucratic Government control. Yet another basis for this co-operation, and perhaps the most significant for both parties, was the importance attached to religious teaching. As this feature has been so influential, we quote the exact statement as it appeared in the memorandum submitted to the Secretary of State for the Colonies in 1925 by the Advisory Committee on Native Education in the British Tropical African Dependencies,[1] this committee itself being one of the most important features and factors in the new policy of co-operation: 'Since contact with civilisation—and even education itself—must necessarily tend to weaken tribal authority and the sanctions of existing beliefs, and in view of the all-prevailing belief in the supernatural which affects the whole life of the African, it is essential that what is good in the old beliefs and sanctions should be strengthened and what is defective should be replaced. The greatest importance must therefore be attached to religious teaching and moral instruction. Both in schools and in training colleges they should be

[1] *Education Policy in British Tropical Africa.* Cmd. 2374. March 1925. H.M.S.O.

accorded an equal standing with secular subjects. Such teaching must be related to the conditions of life and to the daily experience of the pupils.'

Obviously there is room for serious criticism if this statement is intended to cover all that the Christian missionary means by religious teaching, but first let us look at the benefits to Africa and to African education which have followed on the policy of co-operation between Government and missions of which this is one, perhaps the central, component. It has meant that mission schools have held a place, and usually the predominant place, in African education although the school systems have expanded by geometrical rather than arithmetical progression. In the former Gold Coast, for instance, in 1910, some 25,000 children were enrolled in schools; in 1930 there were roughly 60,000; in 1950 nearly 300,000. Between 1930 and 1950 school enrolment in Northern Rhodesia doubled, in Nigeria it trebled, in Kenya quadrupled.[1] Such an expansion would have been impossible by missions alone or by Governments alone. It was made possible by the system of co-operation with its corollary of grants-in-aid by which aided schools were regarded as filling a place in the public system as important as the schools conducted by Government itself.

Again it must be noted that, although the basis of religious teaching already quoted seems inadequate for an evangelical purpose, it offered the State a way by which, without itself adopting a definite religious philosophy of education, it might enlist the help of those who professed the Christian faith. The State, in what was once called British Africa, could not undertake to provide Christian schools, i.e. schools where staff and curriculum were committed to a Christian position, and yet it was anxious to have such schools in its African territories.

[1] *African History in the Making.* P. 99. Supplement by Mr. W. E. F. Ward.

In this respect it was quite different from the French and Belgian administrations, where the former provided a uniform system of State schools of a secular character and the latter maintained the schools of certain religious orders as its *écoles officielles*. Looking at the dilemma of the Government, it appears that the British solution had many advantages because it ensured that the deeper questions which underlie educational theory and practice, questions of the meaning of human life and discipline and character, need not be evaded. The State could secure the required standard of efficiency without encroaching on the freedom of the teacher whose deepest convictions find scope in the whole life and work of a Christian school.

In spite of the inevitable strains inherent in the policy of co-operation, there is remarkable evidence of the fact that on the whole it was welcomed by all parties over the years. In 1952 there met at Cambridge a Conference on African Education attended by representatives of all the colonial territories in Africa, unofficial and official, African and European, men and women, Christians and Muslims. Its work had been prepared by two study groups of experienced educators from this country which had visited West Africa and East Africa respectively and whose reports formed the basis for the work of the Conference. In its Report [1] the Conference noted that the voluntary agencies in African education had changed and multiplied. Missionary societies had largely given place to self-governing African Churches. The boards and committees involved in school work, denominational or secular, were often just as African in composition as the local Governments. By this date also there had been a very considerable development

[1] *African Education.* Nuffield Foundation and Colonial Office. O.U.P. 1953. (Obtainable from Crown Agents.)

in the recognition of responsibility for education by local authorities as well as by the central Government in each territory. These facts make it all the more significant that the Conference should have reported: 'The most important upshot of the conference on the subject of responsibility and control is the community of view which was expressed . . . that education can be carried on only through an effective partnership between the State and the voluntary agencies'. And it went on to say that two other partnerships were also essential: partnership between Europeans and Africans and between the central Government and local authorities.

Enough evidence has perhaps been given to show how big a part missions have played in bringing African education to its present stage. It is equally necessary to enquire what has happened to the aim and character of the education given in mission schools as a result of the immense involvement of Churches and missions in the educational task in Africa. In the pioneering stage, of course, there was little or no distinction between church and school. The same building probably served both purposes. But that stage soon passed when the day schools set out to serve the needs of the community as a whole and not the local congregation. Then followed the setting-up of standards and the enlargement of the curriculum, the strain of increasing costs, even in the most favourable circumstances never wholly met by Government grants, and the shortage of trained staff. These complications constituted a threat to the Christian quality of the education and to the single-mindedness of the missionary educationist and the African Christian teacher. As time went on and the African Church in one territory after another became responsible for large numbers of schools, the burden was felt by the ministers who had to spend much of their time on their duties as school managers. The Church suffered by comparison. Time, effort and money needed for pastoral care, the training and teaching of the congregation, and evangelistic effort to the outsider were devoted to the schools. Instead of the school building up the Church, it seemed as if the Church was being used to build up the school. It was said that boys and girls leaving school were in danger of finding no vital Church ready to receive them.

Undoubtedly there is room for serious misgivings if we are asked to justify the very large place that education takes in the life of many African Churches. We hear doubts expressed as to the quality of the staff when expansion is pushed rapidly forward. We know also that many African boys and girls leave school without any steady attachment and loyalty to the Church. They have simply gone to the Christian school to secure an education otherwise out of reach. It is true that they have received daily lessons in Scripture and they have participated in school worship. We cannot, however, equate this with Christian education unless we know much more about the school and the teacher. It is in fact a subtle danger in assessing schools to think that we have secured 'religion' by teaching it as a subject on the time-table. We need to look into the character and aims of Christian education before we can say how far and under what conditions it can now play a part in the missionary enterprise at this stage comparable with the part played in the early and pioneering stage.

It may help us in this connection to look back to the Le Zoute Conference of September 1926. This was widely representative of missionary interests in British and non-British Africa. Members of the Phelps-Stokes Commission were present and distinguished Colonial administrators. The Conference had in view the new situation in education following on the Reports of the two Commissions, the policy of co-operation between Government and missions in the British territories in Africa and the establishment of the new Committee at the Colonial Office to co-ordinate and expand educational effort in Africa.

The Le Zoute Conference had no doubt about the importance of education in the missionary programme. Dr. A. W. Wilkie, for instance, carried conviction when he claimed: 'Education is not outside the primary plan of Christian missions, but lies at the very heart of it. It is the finest God-given instrument for the evangelisation and the upbuilding of a new Africa.' But the Conference defined the purpose of education in the following terms: 'The members of the Conference see in Jesus Christ all the elements of human greatness meeting in the perfection of grace and truth . . . to fashion character after the pattern of Christ is to them that definition of the aim of education which, traced out in all its implications, is felt by the consent of our whole nature to be at once the highest and the most comprehensive'.[1]

Now these are tremendous claims. If Christian education can rise to the height of this aspiration and extend to the breadth of this conception, there will be no quarrel as to its essential place in the missionary enterprise. But before we agree to this, we must see what is implied in this definition of purpose. First it implies a teacher with the heart of an evangelist. Granted that education is different in its methods and up to a point different in its aims, the deepest motive of a teacher in a school which can be justly termed Christian must be the desire to share with boys and girls the life in all its fullness which he has found in Christ Jesus. Unless he sees the

---

[1] Smith, E. W.: *The Christian Mission in Africa*. International Missionary Council. 1926. P. 59.

educational process as the means of helping boys and girls to grow up into that fullness the school will not provide that kind of environment and community life which is essential. The Christian teacher is concerned with people not subjects, and the training of their bodies in healthy habits, the enrichment of their minds and their growth in personal responsibility and initiative are all contained in and inspired by the ideal of Christian manhood in the companionship of Christ Himself. It will be noticed that the utilitarian or economic side of education, i.e. education as the means of acquiring proficiency in certain branches of knowledge or skills of a practical or professional kind, is here subordinated to the personal, moral and spiritual character of the pupils in the society of the school and the community. But this does not mean the neglect of the other aspects of education. Professor Jeffreys has shown that the concrete, historical and personal emphasis of Christian truth provides the best approach to all the technical and social problems of our age.[1] The loss of confidence in human control and the need for a planned society based on fellowship, two outstanding features of the situation as Christians see it here or in Africa, both point to the need for a Christian or personalist understanding of education. It is through the personal apprehension of a problem that knowledge is co-ordinated and situations understood. It is in the answer to a concrete situation that persons reveal themselves and act and react on one another. Thus hardly any claim is too high for the Christian school if by this term we understand a Christian fellowship of teachers and pupils committed to Christ and to one another in seeking to build up the kind of community in which there is the fullest interchange of life and knowledge and service.

[1] Jeffreys, M. V. C.: Article in *Religion in Education*. March 1943.

Before we examine this claim more closely we must recognise that in order to approximate in any convincing degree to such an ideal, the extent of missionary responsibilities in African education would require to be drastically revised and limited. According to the best statistics available, the International Missionary Council reported recently that, out of 9 to 10 million primary school children in Africa, 8 million are in mission schools. This expansion has been attained at the expense of quality. Of this there can be no doubt if for no other reason than the lack of Christian teachers, missionary and African, with that understanding of their vocation which is here presupposed. Educational quality has in fact suffered both directly and indirectly because the partnership with Government and the effort to meet the insatiable desire for education from the African side has led to the multiplication of schools and school administration to the neglect of other essential tasks. The recruiting of qualified missionary teachers has fallen far behind the needs. The pastoral duties of ordained missionaries and African ministers have had to take second place where school administration imposed a heavy burden. The appointment of African teachers has exceeded the limits which would be prescribed by the primary requisites of deep Christian conviction and adequate professional and personal training. Consequently the pressure of subjects and examinations, financial returns and reports to Government have damaged the Christian character of the school. If one man has to do the work of two and at the same time raise the standard of an examination subject, it simply means that the more important but less tangible things are neglected. It is the time for personal contacts between teacher and pupils or time for some corporate undertaking by the school in service to the community, or leisure for quiet preparation and recovery of perspective that is lost. The utilitarian aim displaces the cultural or Christian aim. Teachers have less opportunity and less capacity for the contacts which in a truly Christian school are the equivalent of the personal work of the evangelist.

Thus we seem to be driven to conceive of the future activity of the Church in African education along two lines. First, the schools owned and managed by the Church as such or by Boards of Governors representing the Church would be relatively few in number, limited in size, and directed primarily to the needs of the Christian community. In these schools every effort would be made to provide a strong Christian staff both as regards numbers in relation to size and standard of the school and as regards Christian personality. It has been agreed in many discussions of educational policy that the points for such concentration of the Church's interest and commitment might well be the training of teachers, and a few distinctively good secondary boarding schools and girls' boarding schools. These schools and colleges should be union institutions, if at all possible, joining the efforts of several Churches. There is no just cause in Africa for divided Churches competing for a place in the educational system. These union schools or colleges should be able to train a far better type of Christian teacher and leader than the average State school can produce. They can provide some of the teachers who can direct the policy and administer the future system of public education. But such a contribution clearly involves a reduction in the range and size of the Church's educational undertakings and the sooner this condition is realised and accepted the better for the African Church as it has taken over and will take over the responsibilities and opportunities bequeathed to it by the mission from overseas.

The other line of action which has a quite unrealised potential is for the African Church to recruit teachers from overseas and train teachers from its own membership for service in State and private schools in Africa. It may seem remote but none the less practical to think of schools founded by benefactions or merchant companies in Africa which will contribute something distinctive to the State system. All will depend on the headmaster and the staff which he is able to gather round him. For Christians there is room for great initiative in the establishment and management of such schools. The content and aim of the educational system in a territory can be and has been affected by the impact of a few schools of outstanding character, and like the old foundations in this country, they can be quite definitely Christian although the official Church has no rights of ownership or management in them. Here also is a field for service by Christian teachers from the West who have received Christ's call to teach but who, for one reason or another, cannot fulfil the conditions required for missionary service.

Our view of education should correspond with our view of life. If we say and believe that human life aims at wholeness, happiness and freedom, we can state the aim of education in the same terms. As Christian believers we cannot do better than describe the aim of education in the words of our Lord Himself: 'I am come that they might have life and that they might have it more abundantly' (John 10, 10) or, in the translation of the New English Bible, 'I have come that men may have life, and may have it in all its fullness'. Obviously life means more to the Christian teacher than it does to the biologist or the social scientist and yet the Christian conception of life includes the material and social environment as well as the moral and spiritual. We shall not make much of Christian education if we neglect the body and its health and discipline, or the action and interaction of the class and group and community-consciousness which is such a formative influence on individual character and outlook. But, assuming as we must a normal healthy all-round interest in life on the natural and human level, we must go a great deal deeper before we are within sight of life in all its fullness as the Christian sees it.

The first point will be that life for the Christian is the gift of God which we receive in and through a personal relation with Christ. This relation of trust and friendship lies at the centre of the teacher's secret understanding of himself and his vocation, his concern for his pupils and his dreams for his school, and it is by virtue of his sharing the life of Christ, or, as St. Paul has it, the life that is Christ, that the teacher can share life in its fullness with the young and immature. Because of what we must go on to say about the expansion and inclusiveness of that life, it is all the more necessary that we should underline its profound and personal character at the centre of the teacher's own apprehension of the world, in which he and his colleagues and pupils live and move and have their being. We might sum this up by saying that for the Christian teacher Christ is the centre of the universe of knowledge, the reality in and behind the events of every day, and the Lord of all good life. And again life is to be understood in the light of Christ's life and death and resurrection, as life laid down and life raised up, or, in von Hügel's words, 'an eternal life already begun and truly known in part here, though fully to be achieved and completely to be understood hereafter'.[1]

Perhaps it is best at this point to take up the question of religion in education. A religious interpretation of life cannot be attained without a basis of religious teaching. Obviously

[1] Baron von Hügel: *Eternal Life*. T. & T. Clark. 1912. P. 395.

the outline of the Bible story must be taught and well taught if children are to be initiated at any stage into the Christian interpretation of history and the facts of the life of Christ. The Christian school cannot be content with stressing the Christian ideal of manhood or the Christian conception of justice and freedom as the basis of a Christian social ethic. It must communicate so far as it can the fundamental attitude of faith in God through Christ as the secret and the way of life. All this involves teaching in its normal sense. There must be knowledge, but to know God means something far greater, far more exacting and humbling and transforming than religious knowledge. To tell the truth, the very organisation of the school and the teaching of religion as a subject on the time-table is a snare and temptation. Religious teaching can tell us about God. Only God can give us the knowledge of Himself which means 'a fearless life of fellowship with Christ in ever fresh adventures of faith'.[1]

This suggests that even when religion has been taught as a subject on the curriculum with the best arrangements of the material, and methods adapted to the age and stage of the pupil, we are only at the beginning of Christian education. We may have taught some of the words of the language of religion, but to know a living language is to speak it in ordinary conversation, to think in its terms, to understand a fellow-creature by means of it. So with religion. Historical fact or doctrinal statement does not become religious truth without an element of personal experience. In that sense religion cannot be taught by any teacher though it may be expressed in the active convictions of living. It is more often 'caught' from someone we trust or admire though, as we grow up, not without an element of recognition and decision. 'Directly

[1] Hogg, A. G.: *Redemption from this World*. T. & T. Clark. 1924. P. 239.

26

teaching runs ahead of learning it becomes not teaching but cramming, and may even be destructive in its effects on the learner. Even God cannot educate at a speed greater than His children's natural development makes possible and fruitful.' [1] We need to remind ourselves incessantly that it is not what is taught that matters in the long run but what is learnt. And 'learning' is largely a matter of the insight gained in terms of previous experience. This surely is the decisive factor in the whole business for teacher and pupil alike. Where and how does Christian experience intersect with life in the quite normal and commonsense meaning of the word? How does the seemingly exclusive personal relation with Christ which is the heart of Christian Faith expand until it becomes 'the circle whose centre is everywhere and its circumference nowhere'? [2]

The essential thing seems to be to avoid every suggestion that religion can be separated from life. F. R. Barry points out in *The Relevance of Christianity* the evil effects which have followed because religion in the West has lost touch with social life and become sectarian and impoverished. The Christian life has too often been interpreted in such exclusively religious terms that it is now identified with a quite private 'religious' experience, that is, the kind of experience reserved for the few rather odd folk who have been 'converted', or with institutional conformity. Large areas in our common life have broken away from Christian standards so that we have what R. H. Tawney called 'a dualism which has emptied religion of its social content and society of its soul'.[3] The importance of this warning lies in the fact that we have inherited this divided mind. It is part of the secularisation of life in the countries of the West and unfortunately we all contribute to this decep-

[1] Yeaxlee, Basil: *The Approach to Religious Education.* S.C.M. Press. 1931. P. 103.
[2] Williams, Charles: *He came down from Heaven.* Faber & Faber. 1950. P. 94.
[3] Quoted F. R. Barry: *The Relevance of Christianity.* Nisbet & Co. 1931. P. 27.

tion when we accept the separation of any part of life, personal, social, political, intellectual or any other, from its proper centre in God. This goes for religion itself. 'There is no stouter bulwark of the secular temper in public life than a Church which is prepared to assent to the secular view of religion as one of the parallel and independent activities of the human spirit.'[1]

Incidentally we ought to notice that nothing could be more foreign to the African apprehension of the world than the view which separates religion and life. For the African who has escaped the demoralising effects of civilisation there is no distinction of religious and non-religious departments or activities. The divine, such as it was for him, was omnipresent and regulated agriculture and economics as much as law and religion. There were offerings to be made and *tabus* to be observed, but these applied to the building of the house, the planting of the crop, the burning of the bricks, the gathering of the clan, as the natural and the supernatural might at any time intersect. People who know West Africa will not be surprised to be told of the motor bus which instead of carrying only the prosaic licence and registration number had the legend 'Guide me, O thou Great Jehovah', and of the taxi which had the slogan 'For God's sake. Weight 15 cwt. Passengers 5. Think of the Future'. This is not the intentional humour, far less irreverence, which it would be for us. Africans do not distinguish as we do, unless we teach them so, the sacred from the secular, the holy from the commonplace. At any time in any place the two may coalesce and combine. For them too the people and the land are mysteriously connected and the community derives from and includes the ancestors who have gone before and the generations yet to come.

[1] Paton, W.: *The Church and the New Order*. S.C.M. Press. 1941. P. 50 f.

Thus there is no more important aspect of Christian education than to help growing boys and girls to resist the forces of disintegration, to see life steadily and to see it whole. This means that from early years the teaching and practice of the Christian school will link the religious and the non-religious activities and interests of staff and pupils. It will not seek to make everything in life equally and directly a religious question, but it will remember that the environment, both physical and social, is the medium in and through which God approaches and speaks to His children and they do or do not respond to Him. The school will not claim that religion is the whole of experience but that it is the heart of experience. So we will avoid the isolation and frustration of religion by seeking always to let its light and truth enlighten and inspire the rest of the school lessons and activities so that it affects nothing less than the total response of mind and heart and will to the God who is behind all life and in whom life finds its meaning. A characteristic passage from Von Hügel's letters to his niece puts this delightfully: 'Everything we do if we do it simply for God is, here and now, the one means of growing in love for Him. Today it is cooking and scrubbing, tomorrow it may be utterly different. Let us practise a genial concentration upon just the one thing picked out for us by God. It is these things as sent, and when willed and at last loved as sent, that train us for Home, that can form a spiritual home for us even here and now.' [1] The Christian school is not a dull place where everything is religious, but a life in which young people do what they have to do happily and to the best of their ability to the glory of God and in His company. Brother Lawrence says of sanctification what we might properly apply to Chris-

[1] von Hügel: *Selected Letters.* J. M. Dent & Sons. 1928. P. 306.

tian education—'that it does not depend upon changing our works but on doing that for God's sake which commonly we do for our own'.

It is a great mistake to think of education as if it were confined to institutions. The 1925 *Memorandum on Education Policy in British Tropical Africa* mentioned on page 15 was followed ten years later by an equally important paper on *The Education of African Communities* which dealt with the fruitful results of co-operation between schools and other agencies in raising the standards of the community in general. In 1944 the Advisory Committee published its proposals on *Mass Education in African Society*, and the Cambridge Conference, in the discussion of 'Education and the Adult', endorsed the statement: 'At least for the short term, there should be a quite novel concentration of energy and resources upon the tasks of informal education'. 'This', wrote Dr. Max Warren, 'was certainly the most revolutionary sentence spoken during the Conference.'

The close association of church and school and community in Africa is a continuous reminder that society as a whole and the way it lives depends on education. The best schools do not live for themselves but have a sense of mission towards the neighbourhood and seek opportunities to serve it. Nor is the benefit given in one direction only, for the link with the community makes the activity of the school so much more intelligible and purposeful. If the life of the pupils is the unifying factor of the curriculum, that life cannot be understood or fostered without a study of the African community at its best in which men are bound to their fellows in mutual responsibility. The African Church, in the villages and on the land, is a visible community with strong natural ties. In health and sickness, in family life, in planting and harvesting, even when its members travel far for work and wages, its ties of kinship and obligation are amazingly strong. This is the community where the results of education will be seen and tested. If the school-training and instruction is worth while, it will show itself not merely or primarily in the number of efficient clerks or artisans who find work far from their native village, but in the homes and gardens of the people, in their more intelligent use of leisure, in their games and songs, their hobbies, their health, their happiness. And it may well be that the school contributes directly as well as indirectly to the education of adult Africans as the centre of the community, the meeting place for clubs or guilds or co-operative societies, in which case again church and school will be two names for the same working and worshipping group.

At the other end of the educational spectrum are the few centres of higher education. For various reasons missionary activity in education has not followed the Indian pattern in setting up Arts and Science colleges under Christian governing bodies, such colleges being constituent parts of the university system. It was left to Government in British Africa to undertake all higher education, the sole exception being Fourah Bay College in Sierra Leone which was originally founded by the Church Missionary Society in 1827. Other colleges, Legon in Ghana, Ibadan and Nsukka in Nigeria, Makerere in Uganda, the University College of Rhodesia and Nyasaland in Salisbury, were all established quite recently, the oldest of these being Makerere which was opened with a few students in 1922. Of course these are quite incapable of supplying the needs of the territories for men and women with professional qualifications, for administrators and leaders of the new nations. According to Mr P. R. G. Hornsby, writing in *The Scotsman* of 27th March 1961, for a total population of more than 100 million in tropical Africa, that is including Liberia, Congo and French West Africa as well as the former British territories, there were only 12 universities or university colleges with a total student population of 7,500. C. E. Carrington in an article in the *Journal of International Affairs* estimated that in 1953 in Great Britian 17,581 British students proceeded to a first university degree, or one in 2,800 of the population. In India the corresponding number was 46,169 or one in 8,120 of the population. Mr Carrington had no comparable number for graduating students for Nigeria, but he counted all who were studying in Ibadan, and the Nigerian students enrolled in universities in Great Britain, Ireland, Canada and the United States. The total was 1,600 or something less than one in 19,000 of the population. His calculation of the number proceeding to a first degree in 1954 was 300, or one in 100,000 of the population.

The universities cannot expand unless they can be fed far more plentifully from the secondary schools. This seems to be the most serious barrier. Dr. Nkrumah said in 1951, when he came to power, that he wanted 400 teachers from Britain. If he could not get them here he would go to Canada, Australia, America or Europe, but he must get them. In one area of Africa it was reported that there were 34 grammar schools without a single science teacher. Three of the schools were due to begin sixth-form work in January 1961 but had no sixth-form teacher. So the greatest need of all is to improve the secondary schools in order to increase the supply of undergraduates for the African universities.

The need for teachers in Africa is made at a time when this country and particularly Scotland is very short of qualified teachers, and, according to the Report of the Committee on the Supply of Teachers in Scotland (January 1962), the position will become more serious. Because of the 'bulge' in school population and the fact that more pupils remain in school beyond the leaving age, the total school roll which was roughly 887,000 in 1960-61 is likely to exceed 900,000 in 1965-66 and to touch the million mark in 1975. Accordingly the shortage of certificated teachers which was 3,673 in 1960 will rise to 5,000 in 1966 and to 6,500 in 1975. If the school leaving age were raised to 16, a further 5,000 teachers would be needed, and if classes were reduced to 30, some 8,000 additional teachers would be required. Yet, even in face of these facts, the appeal for Christian teachers to volunteer for service in Africa must be made. Our shortages here are as nothing compared with the situation overseas. One small state alone needs for next year's classrooms 400 more teachers than it is producing this year. Another will require 20,000 teachers during the next ten years in order to achieve universal primary education by 1970.[1] The countries which owe their ideas of government and law and education to Britain have a right to be heard when they appeal to us for teachers. And who can be expected to hear the call and to make any sacrifice if not Christian teachers ? The opportunities are tremendous, whether in Christian schools under their own Board of Governors or in Government schools if a man or woman does not feel able to sign on as a missionary. As a result of the Commonwealth Education Conference of 1959 the Government have established a National Council for the Supply of Teachers overseas and it has made it easier for teachers from this country to serve for a period in the young Commonwealth countries with the assurance of re-employment when they return.

Why does it matter that Christians should pay serious attention to this appeal from overseas ? One obvious reason is that,

[1] UNESCO Report.

if we don't answer it from this country, the necessary teachers will be recruited in other countries. If we believe in our educational traditions and their long association with Christian faith and life, this seems a pity. We are throwing away one of the hardest-won and most precious links we have with those countries overseas. But it matters still more if we stop to think what influence the ideas and aims governing the content and system of education can exert on the outlook and character of a people.

It is very difficult for us in Britain to realise how much is at stake in the character of education. We do not understand why some nations take education so seriously. But in other countries where education is regarded as entirely the function of the State, totalitarian ideas are spread and a type of character is formed by the consistent theory and rigid practice of the State schools. The rise of nationalism has coincided with the shift of interest in education from subjects to persons. So in Germany and Japan before the War, the system of education and propaganda (for the two were combined) produced a generation which was ready to die for an idea. In Palestine before partition, Jewish schools and Arab schools, as the Royal Commission showed, were the chief centres of Jewish and Arab nationalism. In Africa the potential importance, and the danger, of the school taking sides in politics has been clearly marked in recent years. In Northern Rhodesia, teachers were warned against taking a stand against Federation in the schools, and the Monckton Commission was unable to visit certain mission schools in Nyasaland because of the intense feeling among the pupils and teachers. The grim struggle in the Southern States of America for and against racial integration shows how the schools are involved. Not long ago the Administrator of the Transvaal said that South Africa must win the fight against the non-white in the classroom in place of losing it on the battlefield. Does not this evidence from so many quarters prove that the pre-suppositions that lie behind an educational tradition and the aims it sets out to achieve are vitally important to the Christian mission in Africa? Whether in the new self-governing territories there is going to be a sensitive public conscience may well be decided in the schools. The future of minorities, the possibility of freedom of worship, the right to voice unpopular opinions, the consciousness of belonging to a universal and not a nationalist Church—these are the sort of questions which a Christian education cannot avoid. Education provides the link between religion and life. The power to stimulate imagination and to inspire a passion for truth, the encouragement of friendships and the search for a just social order—these are among the aims of the Christian school and there is only one Master who can give them life and reality. That is why Christian education has an essential place in the Christian mission.

II

THE INTERACTION OF POLITICS
AND MISSION

'THE starting point of missions is the divine commission to proclaim the Lordship of Christ over all life.' [1] In our discussion of Christian Education we saw how this commission has been discharged in Africa through schools and their impact on the life of the people. We tried to show how education, understood in its full personal sense, provides the link between religion and life. In this lecture we will see how the Church's response to the divine commission is everywhere influenced and often deeply injured by political pressures in Africa and how the Church through its members must seek to bear its witness in the political field.

At first sight the involvement of the Church in the political battle may appear undesirable and indeed dangerous to the purpose of the Christian mission in Africa. That it is dangerous we will at once admit though to refuse the involvement would seem still more detrimental to the Church's witness. Before decribing how in fact the missionary movement in its evangelical as well as its catholic expressions has interfered with Governments and influenced Colonial policies in Africa, we should note how social and political witness is inseparable from evangelism. This is well said in J. V. Taylor's Penguin, *Christianity and Politics in Africa*: 'If the Church in Africa (by

[1] Kagawa, quoted by Kraemer: *The Christian Message in a Non-Christian World.* Edinburgh House Press. 1938. P. 60.

36

which is meant the whole Christian Community spread throughout Africa, but focused, as it must be, in the congregations of the locally organised Churches) gives the impression that God is not concerned with man's social and political affairs, then men will not be very much concerned with such a God. And this is not because men wish to use God for their own ends and demand that His thoughts shall be their thoughts; but if they feel that God cares nothing for the things which vitally affect their daily lives and stir their deepest emotions, they will not easily be persuaded that such a God loves them in any real sense at all.'[1] One reason, then, for our interest in politics, though it must not be regarded as standing by itself, is that we cannot obtain a hearing for the Gospel if it has nothing to say about the struggles and fears, ambitions and evils of which men are most conscious in Africa today—and this applies to the white African as well as the black or brown African. And are they to blame if they turn away from a Gospel which has nothing to say to them in their present historical situation? The God and Father of our Lord Jesus Christ is the God of all history, ancient and modern. As He brought Israel from the land of Egypt so He brought the Philistines from Caphtor and the Syrians from Kir. 'Are ye not as the children of the Ethiopians unto me, O children of Israel, saith the Lord?'[2] Man in history is the object of God's love and that means man in Africa, man in community, man in controversy, man in his involvement in the life of the new nations. This is at least one point of contact, and under certain conditions the most accessible point of contact for the evangelist in Africa at present. It may well be that his best opening is the opening words of the Ten Commandments as freely rendered 'I am the God who

[1] Taylor, J. V.: *Christianity and Politics in Africa*. P. 9.
[2] Amos 9, 7.

has taken revolutionary action in history and brought into being a new nation; any other kind of God is a false one'.[1]

But if that is so, the Church's involvement in social and political affairs is demanded as a part of its witness to God's law and not merely in order to get a hearing for the Gospel. Here we see the same paradox as we find in the case of educational and medical missions. Each has its contribution to make to the evangelical concern of the Church. Christian schools, like Christian hospitals, in countless instances have exercised an enlightening or mellowing or disarming effect which has prepared the way for a hearing and understanding of the Gospel. But we have only to note this and at once we recognise that Christian schools and hospitals exercise this ministry just in so far as they are spontaneous expressions of Christian concern and compassion, having their own integral place in the totality of the Christian witness, and not because they serve another purpose and have an ulterior motive. So it is with social and political witness. If it does not spring out of a genuine concern for the men and women and children involved in a particular social and political situation, if it is not related directly to the Lordship of Christ there and then, it is not genuine but counterfeit and therefore rightly suspect. Thus the Church's mission, just because it arises from a sense of responsibility for people where they are, has involved action on the political level and even the most fervent Evangelicals have urged interference with Governments in social and political affairs. More positively and in terms of our own day, it means, so far as possible, equipping the African Church and its people to meet the tremendous demands made upon them in the whole context of the African revolution.

No sooner have we recognised the necessity of politics than

[1] Taylor, supra. P. 21.

we must emphasise the danger of politics in this connection. The danger is not only that preoccupation with political questions is almost an obsession in our day to the exclusion of other equally vital human interests, but that political involvement may divide the Church and destroy the unity of the fellowship which ought to be supra-racial and supra-national. These are risks which must be taken. A serious effort to find a Christian position or different Christian positions in this field can lead on to a fresh understanding of the need for individual conviction and penitence and consecration. 'Part of our social witness itself', wrote William Temple, 'must be the perpetual warning that whatever the social and economic system, human selfishness will find ways of exploiting it unless it be extirpated by the power of the Gospel; and this cannot be carried out wholesale; it is done now for this soul, now for that; it is the essence of individual conversion. The Gospel itself impels us to the task of social witness; our social witness leads us and all who hear us back to the Gospel.'[1] That is the best we can hope for as a result of such action but we must not understate the critical dilemma of the Church in Africa: 'A religion which is not related positively to the total developing life of the community will never do for Africa. But neither will a social Gospel busily engaged in a programme of improvement which leaves the deep personal levels of human nature untransformed. The heart of the matter is the urgent need for a Church in Africa which is both supernatural and responsible, in the full meaning of both those words.'[2]

It may be a surprise to those who think of missionary work as exclusively evangelical, in the sense of winning individual souls through preaching, to learn that the Evangelical as well

[1] William Temple: *Social Witness and Evangelism*. Epworth Press. 1943. P. 9.
[2] Taylor, op. cit. P. 20.

as the Catholic Missions were much concerned with political questions in the early days of the missionary movement in Africa. In the nineteenth century, before the 'Scramble for Africa', that is before, say, 1885, Africa, with the exception of the West Coast and what is now called South Africa, was little known to the West. The missionary penetration of East and Central Africa followed quickly on Livingstone's death in 1873. The Universities Mission to Central Africa had indeed made a first attempt to found a station in Nyasaland ten years before that, as a result of Livingstone's famous appeal in the Senate House in Cambridge. That attempt failed and it was left to the Free Church of Scotland and the Church of Scotland to pioneer the way for the Gospel in that part of Africa. The Church Missionary Society had been busy on the East Coast even earlier though they did not reach Uganda until the middle seventies. It was a time of intense activity in the missionary field. 'By the end of 1881 seven different missions were established within striking distance of what is now Northern Rhodesia.' [1]

It is not the history of those missions to which attention is drawn but to the fact that missionary occupation preceded commerce and Government, and was largely instrumental in bringing about the arrival of these other Western secular influences and agencies. As Roland Oliver shows conclusively, [2] missions were a factor of immense importance in the expansion of European interests in Africa in the latter part of the nineteenth century when the interior of the continent was opened up to the outside world. In Nyasaland the Scottish missions directly and indirectly exercised a decisive influence on the declaration of a British Protectorate. To begin with

[1] Taylor & Lehmann: *Christians of the Copperbelt*. S.C.M. Press. 1961. P. 28.
[2] Roland Oliver: *The Missionary Factor in East Africa*. Longmans, Green & Co. 1952.

they set up residential stations or communities to which Africans gathered for work, for safety, for mutual support. Missions in the early period were not trying to draw Governments into Africa. Nor were they trying to secure Government support for their work among Africans. But all the time by correspondence, by deputation and education among their home supporters, and by their concern with the effects of the Slave Trade, they were building up a body of enlightened and potentially influential public opinion at home.

So when the Arabs attacked the Livingstonia Company's Trading Post at Karonga in 1887, the Scottish Churches were soon mobilised to appeal for support for the Company. The story of how Scottish interests besieged the Government is well known. Four bulky volumes of signatures were presented to Lord Balfour of Burleigh; and Lord Salisbury, the Prime Minister, welcomed the pressure of Scottish interests. Perhaps the concern of the home Churches in checking the slave trade would not have been enough, but the presence of Portuguese in the Zambesi area, their indulgent attitude to slavery and their claims to Southern Nyasaland combined to carry the Government. Nyasaland was declared a British Protectorate. So, too, in Uganda it was the pressure of the Church Missionary Society, its contact with public opinion at home, together with the financial exhaustion of the Imperial British East Africa Company, which forced the Government to intervene and finally to declare a Protectorate there. Again, it might have hesitated longer but for the threats of German expansion in East Africa. By such a strange mixture of philanthropy and business acumen, missionary zeal and diplomacy, the expansion of the British Empire thus proceeded. The missionary and the missionary constituency in this country had a large share in this. There was no hesitation then about political

41

action. The missionaries in Nyasaland as in Uganda realised quite rightly that the territory could not remain independent. It would be brought under the rule and protection of one country or another in Europe. They preferred their own. What we have to notice is that instead of trade following the flag, trade followed the Gospel and the flag followed both.

At a later point in the history of East Africa missionary intervention was again directly responsible as a factor in Government policy. In the pioneering days colonial policy had been in favour of missionary work. Tributes were paid to the effects of residence and training on the mission stations. Colonial officials could not ignore the signs of social progress in and around these settlements: the permanent buildings, well-engineered roads and bridges, printing presses, workshops, orchards and vegetable gardens. They also looked to the missions for trained artisans, clerks and teachers. But at a later date, as Governments extended their interests into fields which had been the prerogative of missions, and as missions became more conscious of the disparity and conflict between the Gospel and modern Western civilisation, relations between Government and missions, Church and State, were often difficult. In the past fifty years, as a result of the organisation which followed the World Missionary Conference of 1910, there has grown up an effective means of collaboration and co-operation between Government and missions, especially in the field of education. But that has not prevented the missionary factor from operating sometimes in opposition to Government policy. One outstanding instance concerned the use of African labour on European farms in Kenya. The story is told in the book already mentioned[1] and still more fully in Miss Perham's life of Lord Lugard.[2] This time it was the initiative of

[1] Roland Oliver, op. cit. P. 247.
[2] Margery Perham: *Lugard*. Collins. 2 vols. 1956, 1960.

Dr. J. H. Oldham as Secretary of the International Missionary Council which made the difference. He was in constant touch with the missionaries in Kenya, notably with Dr. J. W. Arthur of Kikuyu and the Alliance of Protestant Missions. When after the First World War General Northey, the Kenya Governor, began to issue instructions to his administrative officers to see that the chiefs supplied the labour necessary for the European farms, it was evident to the missionaries in Kenya that something not unlike compulsory labour would soon follow. The missionaries challenged the Government on the issue. They argued that such policy would drain off the necessary proportion of male Africans from the villages with injury to their home life and their crops. They objected to the increase in native taxation which had the same effect of inducing Africans to work for wages.

When representations to the Secretary of State failed to draw a satisfactory reply, the missionaries were able to put the matter in Dr. Oldham's hands. By his exceptional knowledge and wisdom, his wide contacts in both Church and State, and his capacity for recognising when a particular question had to be treated as fundamental, Dr. Oldham got together and presented to Government a strong memorandum on 'Labour in Africa and the Principles of Trusteeship' supported and signed by an influential group of men and women of all political parties.[1] The Memorandum raised issues which were to be the subject of the Ormsby-Gore Commission of 1924, and the Hilton Young Commission of 1928, of which Dr. Oldham himself was a member. When the Governor issued a new circular instructing the District Officers to discourage Africans from growing cash crops in the Reserves, Dr. Oldham was again in touch with the Archbishop of Canterbury and through him with the Secretary of State. Though

[1] Roland Oliver, op. cit. P. 252 f.

43

the Government in Kenya modified its policy and issued a directive that officials were not to recruit labour for European farms, the central issue had not been faced, namely, the relative claims of the different communities in East Africa and their place in the future development of the country, the very issue which has reached the stage of decision just recently.

The opportunity for further action came as a result of a question raised by the Government of India as to the representation of the Indian immigrant community in Kenya on the Legislative Council. When it was suggested that Indians and Europeans should have a common roll, the Europeans in Kenya raised a very bitter protest, even going to the extreme of planning to kidnap the Governor. Missionary opinion at the outset was divided, Indian missionaries naturally differing from their Kenya colleagues on the question. Here again Dr. Oldham's influence was decisive. He reconciled the differences within the missionary constituency and persuaded a delegation from India that the best course was to press for a declaration by the British Government that the interests of the great African majority should, in case of conflict, take precedence over other interests and that the grant of responsible government to any immigrant minority was not compatible with this policy. When in 1923 the Government issued the White Paper, *Indians in Kenya*, it contained the statement: 'Primarily Kenya is an African territory and His Majesty's Government think it necessary definitely to record their considered opinion that the interests of the African natives must be paramount and that if and when those interests and the interests of the immigrant races should conflict, the former should prevail. . . . As in the Uganda Protectorate, so in the Kenya Colony, the principle of trusteeship for the natives, no less than in the Mandated Territory of Tanganyika is unassailable.' During the next few years, Dr. Oldham, acting with and for the missionary interests, was to have a very close connection with political developments in East Africa. The missionary conscience was quickened to political action not only by concern for the total life of the African people but by a sense that British Colonial policy must be judged and modified to accord more closely with the principles of the Christian Faith.

Such illustrations of intervention will show that, in defence of backward and underprivileged peoples, the missionary body were for the most part convinced that their obedience had political implications. Indeed, one of the significant features of the World Missionary Conference of 1910 was the place given to the subject of Missions and Governments and this concern was taken up by the International Missionary Council and the various National Missionary (later, Christian) Councils and Conferences which came into being after the First World War. The relation of Missions and Governments has now become the issue of Church and State and behind the change of name lies the drastic and dramatic change in the situation on the so-called mission fields which we recognise today. Amidst all the immense and bewildering varieties of circumstance and stage of development the two constant factors already achieved or plainly emerging are the autonomous Church in place of the mission, and the successor State instead of the Colonial Government. Although there has been no time as yet to see what the stable relationship will be (if indeed there is any chance of a stable relationship) it is clear that the Church in Africa, whether in West or East or South, in Ghana and Nigeria, in the Union, in Nyasaland, Rhodesia, Kenya or Uganda, will have to stand on its own ground and deal with its own Government. This means at one and the same time more difficulty and danger in entering the political field, more dubiety and possibility of division on political issues, and yet the same or even greater need for the Church to prove its concern with and intelligent grasp of political issues which affect the whole life of its people.

Matters are made more difficult by the fact that the missionary, in spite of himself, still is or is taken to be a political influence, if not an agent of the Colonial power. The missionary is a servant of the local Church, subject to its courts, and at the most a sharer in the decisions which the Church takes. When the agenda of Kirk Session, Presbytery, or Synod raises matters of Church and State, he must take a subordinate part because he is not a national of the country and he does not know from the inside what it means to be a member of the African community. Yet the missionary, because of his skin and his country of origin, may be held responsible and has often been blamed for not intervening more boldly, for not criticising the policy of the Colonial Government. Except in West Africa, where Europeans are so few and so temporary in proportion to the African population that they hardly count in Government or political life, the relation of Church and State is further complicated by race. The Church itself is divided, either by constitution or in day-to-day living, by barriers of race. The missionary is therefore liable to incur suspicion from either and sometimes from both sides if he has, or if he fails to have, a definite position on political questions.

Events in Nyasaland, particularly after the declaration of a state of emergency in March 1959, throw a vivid light on this confusion of politics, Church and missionary, and show how difficult, if not impossible, it is to disentangle them. In this case, although individual missionaries at various times openly declared their sympathy with the aims of the Nyasaland African Congress, most of them took no part in local politics at all, and some expressed a cautious, if not critical, attitude towards Congress. The Church of Central Africa Presbyterian, many of whose elders and members were members or officials of the Congress, had more than once made public statements which expressed its concern over the imposition of Federation against the will of the people and called for an assurance from Government that the way was open for Nyasaland to advance towards self-government. Yet the Government of the Federation, through its Information Service, failed to distinguish the Church of Scotland from the Church in Nyasaland and showed no understanding of the fact that it was the Church of the country and not a few missionaries with which the Government had to deal. Of course the Church of Scotland through its General Assembly had from 1952 onwards urged that full consideration should be given to African opinion and that no scheme should be adopted without the consent and co-operation of the Africans. Yet the position reached by the Church in Nyasaland was entirely its own and one can safely say that, had the Church of Scotland expressed quite different views on federation, the Church in Nyasaland would still, however reluctantly, have expressed the same opposition.

In Northern Rhodesia, missionaries have incurred suspicion and criticism from both Government and the African Church. In 1935 the Missionary Conference took exception to the composition of the Committee of Enquiry set up by Government after disturbances on the Copperbelt. The Governor thereupon chose to attend the Conference and reprimand the missionaries for associating themselves 'with overt criticism of the activities of Government'. The same day the Acting President of the Conference replied: 'We claim the right to criticise when criticism is obviously deserved and our criticism is offered in kindness and with a desire to help both Europeans and Natives and also the Government. We think it does not quite deserve the castigation which it has received this morning'.[1] Yet the same careful study of the Church and community on the Copperbelt reports the fact that a great many Africans were disillusioned and disappointed by the failure of the mission churches to speak out on political questions, notably on federation: 'The Church let us down over federation'.[2] In fact the federation issue seems to have been regarded by many as the ultimate test of the integrity of European Church leaders. 'The fact that thousands of Europeans, in Southern as well as Northern Rhodesia, voted against federation; the fact that many of the white Christians sincerely believed that federation was in the best interests of Africans as well as Europeans; or the fact that some Church leaders did protest against the overriding of African opposition—these seem hardly to have affected their verdict.'[3] Africans remembered only that their European friends, including the leaders of the Churches, had not fought with them over the federation issue.

This last quotation opens our eyes to the real gravity of the question of politics in today's Africa—and, remember, we are concerned here with the Gospel and the mission of the Church and not with political problems and solutions for their own sake. Whatever our politics in this country now or on election day, we have to take serious note of the fact that not only the missionary agency but the African Church and the Gospel itself suffers from the tie-up with the white man, and his association with the Colonial power. 'Christianity itself is beginning to be regarded as an agency for weakening African

[1] Taylor and Lehmann, op. cit. P. 160.
[2] Taylor and Lehmann, op. cit. P. 163.
[3] Taylor and Lehmann, op. cit. P. 153 f.

resistance.' [1] From a group of essays written by school children in Northern Rhodesia the following quotations are made: 'Christianity was brought by white people to conquer Africans'. 'Livingstone came to make Africans soft.' [2] Christianity is thus regarded as essentially a white man's religion: 'All churches in the world help white people only'. 'Jesus was born by a white woman; we cannot follow him.' [3]

No doubt these fantastic falsehoods are the result of propaganda from outside, by radio and the Press, and by contacts with Communist and quasi-Communist ideas. That recognition, however, in no way lessens the significant fact that these ideas take root very easily in Africa, even in the minds of African Christians. The ominous thing is that by the connection, almost identification of politics and race, practically any question on which Africans and Europeans feel at all deeply can become a political question and every political question is liable to become a racial issue. 'The issue of federation', says one observer, 'has changed the relationship of employer and employed, of administration and administered, to one of black and white.' [4] We might add that the political question in Africa today, and not only on the Copperbelt but in East, South and Central Africa, and not impossibly in West Africa too, can work the same wicked transformation in the relations of the European Christian, missionary or non-missionary, and the African Christian.

Before we condemn the African standpoint as wholly wrong we should remember that Christianity, like the religion of Israel from which it emerged, has always been and claims to be the faith of a community. We get into all kinds of diffi-

---

[1] Taylor and Lehmann, op. cit. P. 154.
[2] Taylor and Lehmann, op. cit. P. 156.
[3] Taylor and Lehmann, op. cit. P. 190.
[4] Taylor and Lehmann, op. cit. P. 137.

culty and unbelief if we seek the Kingdom of God not for the sake of His sovereign grace and righteousness but for our own sake or for society's. Yet the Gospel claims to be the Word of Reconciliation and our Lord Himself encouraged men to apply this practical test when He said, 'By this shall all men know that ye are my disciples if ye have love one to another'. African Christians use this simple criterion when they look at the Church or the Churches. Is it effective as an institution in society? The 'this worldliness of the African Church'[1] is quite in accordance with the traditional African view of religion. The African, until he comes in contact with the divided mind of the West does not separate the different aspects of life into specialised departments of religion, law, politics, economics, industry and so on. To him, sacred and secular, material and spiritual, natural and supernatural are closely and mutually implied and involved. This view would not seem so strange to us if we had not been brought up in a 'schizophrenic Western culture (built paradoxically upon a materialistic technology and the Christian faith)'.[2] As it is, our tendency is to be content with Churches in which Christianity is so spiritualised that it loses its social content. It is hardly recognisable as 'far the most materialistic of the great religions'[3] and we are never quite clear about the connection between religion and politics.

To this extent we are ill-equipped for the task of understanding the problem in its full dimensions, and, unfortunately, the foreign mission has too often failed to prepare the Church in Africa to work out its own proper approach to politics. The old evangelical preaching had very marked limi-

[1] Taylor and Lehmann, op. cit. P. 121.
[2] Taylor and Lehmann, op. cit. P. 275.
[3] William Temple: *Personal Religion and the Life of Fellowship*. Longmans, Green & Co. 1926. P. 17.

tations at this point for it was more concerned with individual salvation interpreted as a private transaction between the soul and its Maker, a salvation issuing in a strict individual and family code of morality but with no specific guidance for the wider problems of society. Hence surely Mr. J. V. Taylor [1] is right in saying that when the modern social and industrial revolution invaded Africa it found the majority of Christians of all races dangerously unprepared. The danger was accentuated by the fact that while educated men (and that meant the younger men, educated for the most part at mission schools with or without a college course) were ready to give wholehearted loyalty to the national Congress party or its equivalent, many of the older African ministers were so anxious to keep the Church out of politics that they had no guidance to give these younger men. The gulf between the old and young which is a fact of significance in every society but most of all in societies undergoing a process of revolutionary change thus becomes most serious for the Church in Africa.

It is most difficult to assess the political involvement of African Christians. In Nyasaland the Congress Party commanded the support of most Africans inside as well as outside the Church before as well as after the emergency declared in 1959. From Northern Rhodesia it is reported 'that the majority in any congregation on the Copperbelt (with two exceptions) are likely to be members of both Church and Congress with equal conviction and regularity'.[2] On the other hand it has to be admitted that, very often, the officials in Congress are not active Church members. Some are just 'lapsed' Christians, others have been disciplined, and others again are hostile

[1] Taylor: *Christianity and Politics in Africa*. P. 8.
[2] Taylor and Lehmann, op. cit. P. 168.

to the Church. Yet, if as seems likely, many of the leaders and the vast majority of the members of the African political parties are still Church members and owe their education to Christian schools, there is still time to recover the vital connection between the Church and the national spirit which has caught the imagination and the enthusiasm of the emergent African. Meantime there are outstanding examples of Africans whose Christian convictions have led them into politics, some in opposition, some in office.

That Christians should play their part in politics is vital not simply for the sake of the Church and to secure a hearing for the Gospel. It is vital for the future of Africa. In the Colonial era the relation of missions and Governments or Church and State was not easy but the tension had a healthy influence. It was good for Africa that the Church from time to time was able to arouse the conscience of the State. It was also necessary for the State to remind the Church that it had a duty and responsibility to carry out for all its citizens, Church members or not, a duty and responsibility which the Church could not discharge and of which it was woefully ignorant. Now in the successor or autonomous States in Africa the need and opportunity is still more important. In days of perfervid nationalism when it is all too easy for Africans to believe that the end of the Colonial era will immediately and inevitably bring harmony, prosperity and freedom, the Church has to correct the idolatry of the nation and the Utopian pretensions of political propaganda. To do this will mean taking risks. It is not characteristic of new nations to be tolerant of criticism. Democracy in Africa may mean something different from what it means in this country. It is possible that one-party Government will try to stifle all criticism of itself and that minority opinion, whether in the Church or outside, will not be allowed. If so it will be all the more necessary for Christians in Africa to be able to look to Christians in other lands for guidance and help as they try to play their part as individuals in the public life and service of their country.

Whether in one situation or another, it is clear that the Church is rendering a great service to the State when it provides the men and women who, by their integrity, discernment and courage, are fitted to take an active part in the social and political life of their people. The pace of political change is beyond calculation. In 1960 sixteen African countries obtained their independence. Sir Andrew Cohen, who was the British representative on the Trusteeship Council at the United Nations, estimated that soon the African group in the General Assembly would be the largest of any, nearly equal in numbers to the West European and pre-war Commonwealth countries and the Soviet bloc combined.[1] The outside reaction to these dramatic changes may be cynicism or despair. We ask how can these things be? Political constitutions are worth little if there are no people to make them work. But is that not the opportunity for the Church to send its members out into the rough and tumble of public affairs and to give them at least some preliminary guidance and sense of responsibility which will enable them to strengthen their brethren and to provide the spirit that is essential to the health of the body politic?

Here we must distinguish, as best we can, between the Church as an official body, meeting for worship and fellowship, a corporate body with its courts and officers and official statements—all this on the one hand—and the Church as the Christian people in their life and witness in the world. The Church, then, in the former sense has to provide inspiration

[1] *International Affairs*. October 1960.

and guidance to its members with a view to their participation, among other things, in political life. The consensus of opinion in the non-Roman Churches is that Christians should not form a political party. There should be no attempt at a Christian party so-called. Rather the Christian fellowship should aim at inspiring its members to accept their responsibilities as citizens and leave them to attach themselves to different political parties. In Africa it would be a blessing if Christians, as Mr. Taylor suggests, could acquire experience in local government, in co-operative societies and trade unions. In these fields as in the social services of Government, in political journalism, radio, etc., standards can be set and experience gained which is of immense value in national life and politics. As the Evanston Report on the Laity reminded us, the real battles of the Faith are fought in these secular fields and the Church does not need to enter these spheres because it is already there in the persons of its laity. But the laity are mostly untrained and unsupported. The Church as an institution is not adapted to the real needs of the lay world.[1] African ministers are no more fitted than our ministers are to give such training. The best means so far seems to be the provision of lay training centres such as the Evangelical Academies on the Continent. A beginning has been made in Central Africa by setting up the Ecumenical Centre at Mindolo in the Copperbelt. Other Christian Councils are seeking to do something similar but on a more modest scale within their own resources.

Perhaps the best thing we could do to help these Churches would be to let them see European Christian laymen at work in all kinds of professions and occupations, men and women

---

[1] W. A. Visser 'tHooft and J. H. Oldham: *The Church and its Function in Society*. Allen & Unwin. 1937. Pp. 192-199.

such as Oversea Service aims to gather in its training courses, 'seculars' and not professional missionaries, technicians, Government servants, trade unionists, journalists, each of them qualified in their own jobs but doing them as their Christian service and openly linking themselves by one means or another (here the Overseas Fellowship has its part to play) with African fellow Christians and with the Church of the country.

This is where we are driven back again on the question of politics and race as they impinge on the Church. There is a danger, writes a missionary in Nyasaland, no doubt with an echo of something said nearer home, that certain Churches may appear to be but the several political parties at prayer. The crisis in Nyasaland to an alarming extent split the Churches along racial lines. The United Federal Party was almost entirely European. The Malawi Congress Party, with the exception of a few Europeans, mostly missionaries, was entirely African— and the Churches were likewise divided. European and African Christians, on the whole, both reverted to type. The European Christian seemed no more able to preserve fellowship across racial lines than was the African. The two congregations linked with the Church of Scotland had been on the point of joining up with the Church of Central Africa but the political struggle reversed that movement. It is encouraging to know, however, that last year, after the elections and the return of Dr. Banda's party by an overwhelming majority, these congregations in Blantyre and Zomba applied to Synod and were received as English-speaking congregations of the Church of Central Africa Presbyterian.

The question of the Church, one might say, the very test of the existence of the true Church, is whether it can demonstrate to the world a living fellowship which bridges the gap between the races. There is nothing in Africa which can so witness to the divine power and presence as the reconciliation of black and white in such a relationship that they can confess their faults to one another and join together in an effort to unite their bitterly divided communities. This means finding something in common which Africans and Europeans outside the Church do not themselves experience. It means going further and often going against the conventions, even the convictions of society. It means for the African Christian that he runs the risk of being shunned and distrusted by his own people. On the Copperbelt there is deep suspicion of Africans who are on close and friendly terms with Europeans. Even to be visited by a missionary may be an embarrassment in a strongly anti-European setting. African ministers are frequently regarded as informers by their own people because they work in fellowship with missionaries. The European Christian, too, has to run the gauntlet of public opinion in his job, or in his trade union, or at the Club if he espouses the African cause and associates with Africans socially and informally.

The authors of *Christians of the Copperbelt*, to which frequent reference has been made, point out that African Christians are now discussing seriously the pros and cons of separate African and European Churches. This would seem at first sight due only to disillusion and bitterness. African Christians indeed have much experience of segregation in English-speaking Churches, though with the exception of the Dutch Reformed Church, Jehovah's Witnesses and the All-African Churches, the different denominations are theoretically open to all races. But further examination shows that this is not simply a reaction against the colour bar. There is a good deal to be said for separate Churches in an area where there are marked differences of race. Where there are wholly African congregations with their own ministers and church courts, the different views of Africans and Europeans can be separately provided for. Missionaries can be set aside for whole-time African work. Services of worship, forms of discipline, social customs congenial to Africans and not to Europeans can be employed. The financial arrangements can be different for African and European. Yet in spite of these strong arguments, and the attractive possibilities of an All-African Church, such as the small separatist group of the Roman Catholic Church, the Bana ba Mutima,[1] the balance lies with the inclusion of both European and African Christians in one Church under one constitution. The United Church of Central Africa in Rhodesia was constituted after this pattern in 1958. This brought the European congregations on the Copperbelt into the same Church as the neighbouring African congregations and those distant rural congregations that had sprung from the work of the London Missionary Society, and the Livingstonia Mission of the Church of Scotland. In Kenya the Presbyterian Church of East Africa is also inter-racial, including European, African and also Asian Christians.

The constitution of these Churches represents only the beginning of inter-racial fellowship. What is possible in Synod and Presbytery has to be made real in local congregations. The obstacles to be overcome are very real, and personal relations which grow into real friendships between black and white are rare indeed. Yet this is one of the first fruits which by God's appointment and the blessing of the Spirit, become the growing point of the Church's life. The first fruits represent what is to follow, and they carry with them the dedication of the rest. The Church proves itself a unique institution when Christian opinion can enter into and yet transcend politics; when the

[1] Taylor and Lehmann, op. cit. Pp. 106-108, 113, 167.

African becomes part of a supra-racial and world-wide fellowship wherein the deepest differences are recognised and yet in a measure reconciled. It is easy for us at this distance to say this, but without some vivid experience of the offence of the colour bar we only say 'Peace, peace' when there is no peace. If African Christians are to establish the right relation between their faith and their action in politics they need a flexibility and willingness to forgive, indeed a grace which is beyond human resources. Moreover they and we alike must learn with Karl Barth that, important as they are, politics are better taken as a sport, although a serious sport, and that 'God alone has the right and the possibility of being completely serious'.[1]

[1] Charles West: *Communism and the Theologians.* S.C.M. Press. 1958. P. 209.

III

GOSPEL AND CHURCH IN
AFRICAN SOCIETY

MANY supporters of 'foreign missions' regard questions of education and politics with which we have been concerned in the two previous lectures as secondary and peripheral. They want to make certain that the Church's missionary enterprise is first of all concerned with the proclamation of the Gospel and the encounter of man with God. With this fundamental motivation there can be no difference of opinion if we take seriously Christ's statement of His own purpose and His commission to His disciples. We can argue, however, that through the Church's concern with education and with politics men are placed in a position where Christ Himself meets them in His judgment and His grace. This is a crucial question to which we must return. Meantime the ground covered in the previous discussion helps us at least to see how the impact of the Church and the Gospel occurs within the larger, more confused and confusing context of historical events in Africa, and how the response of Africans is to be understood best within that same context. 'Considered historically [1] and sociologically', writes J. V. Taylor, 'the communication of the Gospel is a matter of culture contacts; theologically it is more than that—"and in that *more* lies all her hopes of good".' In other words 'Missionaries have taken to Africa not "the pure milk of the Gospel"—it is part of what theologians call "the scandal of particularity" that they do not know what it is— but a complex culture which it is perhaps easiest to call "Chris-

[1] J. V. Taylor: *The Growth of the Church in Buganda*. S.C.M. Press .1958. P. 253.

59

tian-western" in which the faith is inextricably interwoven with the techniques and values of a civilisation which it has itself helped to create'.[1]

It is important to grasp this point. Without claiming that missionaries or missionary societies have been exempt from ordinary human failings we can see that much of the criticism of missionary effort and much of the disappointment with which a realistic account of the Church in Africa is received would be obviated if this complication were kept in mind. The message as *heard* by the African is not a purely religious message. The response he makes to it is not just a religious response. There may be, and by God's grace there must be, an encounter between a man and his Maker when the Church takes the Gospel to Africa. Yet the missionary movement, even where missionaries were the first white men to make contact with Africans, was only one aspect of so-called Christian-western culture, a culture which was an amalgam of highly diversified and often inconsistent elements. It is true that Western civilisation in its expansion to the East and Africa was never completely secular, never without a deeper background of belief or without some concern for the eternal destiny of man. 'For two hundred years, dating from the beginning of the da Gaman era, our world-storming Western forefathers made a valiant attempt to propagate abroad the whole of our Western cultural heritage including its religious core as well as its technological rind; and in this they were surely well-inspired; for every culture is a "whole" whose parts are subtly inter-dependent, and to export the husk without the grain may be as deadly as to radiate the satellite electrons of an atom without the nucleus.'[2]

[1] F. B. Welbourn: *East African Rebels*. S.C.M. Press. 1961. P. 170.
[2] Arnold J. Toynbee: *Civilisation on Trial*. 1948. P. 84 f.

In fact, however, the rest of the world has accepted some elements in Western culture and rejected others. Whether owing to the failure of the West to live up to its own declared principles or owing to the resistance of other cultures and religions to the Christian revelation, the West has exported its technology, its 'know-how', and its democratic and political ideas to many lands without establishing their Christian origin and foundation. In spite of the Church's efforts in Christian education—and we have seen that they are by no means insignificant—Africans too have often adopted a secularised version of Western civilisation in which education is sought only for its economic and utilitarian values, and politics are largely a reaction to the colour bar and technology is a substitute for religion.

In the study of the contact of the West with Africa the establishment and growth of the Independent Churches deserves particular attention. By 'Independent' is meant originating in Africa (though they may have been inspired by some church pattern from overseas) and led by Africans. These Churches are to be distinguished therefore from Churches which have a missionary, that is foreign missionary, origin, though the latter may be equally self-governing and led by Africans. The Independent Churches, with perhaps only one exception,[1] are separate or separated Churches which have no organic connection with any of the Roman or non-Roman Christian communities outside Africa. These Independent Churches are of value in showing what the African, when left to himself, makes of the Church and Christianity. Moreover these Churches multiply and grow in such profusion that they must express a spontaneous movement of African thought and life which deserves the notice of the Younger Churches

[1] The African Greek Orthodox Church.

as they seek to become truly indigenous. The Independent Churches for their own sake deserve sympathetic attention. J. V. Taylor writes of the deep African rejection of complete Westernisation and instances the African view of man as part of nature in distinction from the European view of man in control of nature, and the African valuation of man and his work and leisure in preference to the European assumption that man is only of value because of his function in the world's work. 'Such deep spiritual rejection of these and other aspects of modern Western culture, for all that Africa has been, and is still, fascinated by the white man's technical achievements, is something that must be taken into account if we are to have the slightest hope of building together the emergent African peoples, with the Asian and European minorities, into one multi-racial community.' [1] It is here that the study of the Independent Churches assumes more than a passing significance.

Pioneer work on this subject was done in South Africa by Professor (now Bishop) Sundkler.[2] In an appendix to his book he gave a list of 877 bodies classed as Native Separatist Churches by the Secretary for Native Affairs. Dr. Max Warren in 1954 [3] mentions that there are more than thirteen hundred different sects in South Africa. But the phenomenon of these Churches is not confined to those parts of Africa where it can be understood as a natural reaction to apartheid and the white man's rejection of the African as a fellow-citizen. Dr. Parrinder [4] has given a most instructive account of Independent Churches in West Africa where many of the same features are present though in this region they cannot be explained as reaction to conquest. With Mr. Welbourn's *East African Rebels*,

[1] J. V. Taylor: *Christianity and Politics in Africa*. P. 103 f.
[2] B. J. M. Sundkler: *Bantu Prophets in South Africa*. Lutterworth Press. 1948.
[3] *Revival. An Enquiry*. Max Warren. S.C.M. Press. 1954. P. 27.
[4] G. Parrinder: *Religion in an African City*. O.U.P. 1953.

to which reference has already been made, we have a large-scale study of four individual Independent Churches in Uganda and Kenya, and Dr. Parrinder's work is now supplemented by Dr. Debrunner's *Witchcraft in Ghana* with its account of the African healing Churches.[1]

One curious feature which is common to many of these Churches is the rejection of Western medicine. In Nigeria both foreign and native medicines are forbidden in these Churches. In South Africa one of the best known of the Zulu prophets, Isaiah Shembe, received his call after a terrifying experience when lightning killed his best ox and he was left with the scar of a burn on his thigh. When a Zulu leech came to cure him, Shembe answered 'Jehovah has revealed to me that I must not be healed by medicine, but only through His Word'.[2] To many of these Christians, dependence on medicine is equivalent to the worship of Satan. One of the Independent Churches in Uganda is called the Society of the One Almighty God. The date of its separation from the Native Anglican Church is uncertain but it must have been about 1914. By 1921 census figures gave 91,740 members in the Kingdom of Buganda alone. The principal feature of this Society was its rejection of medicine for man and beast, indeed the name of the group, the Society of the One Almighty God, was derived from its insistence that we must trust in God alone. For Mugema, the founder, 'to combine Christianity with medicine was to try to worship God and Mammon at the same time'. ' He appreciated deeply the importance of obedience to the one God. His rejection of medicine insisted—whether rightly or wrongly—that this ideal had been distorted by a purely Western acceptance of the cult of health, a

[1] H. Debrunner: *Witchcraft in Ghana*. Kumasi Presbyterian Book Depot. 1960.
[2] B. J. M. Sundkler, op. cit. P. 110.

cult which might readily oust faith in the One Giver of health.'[1] This rejection is all the more remarkable when we give due weight to the overwhelming effect of the white man's technical achievements on Africans and the insistence on health and hygiene in schools.

Over against this opposition to medicine which to them meant paganism, old or new, the Independent Churches set prayer and healing through prayer. The prayer of faith was believed to cure all diseases, to protect the believer from accidents, to enable sterile women to bear children,[2] Sundkler [3] writes that while the Roman Church offers grace through its sacraments and the Protestant relies on teaching and preaching, the Independent Church of the Zionists is an Institute of Healing. Healing is the very pivot of its activity. The usual answer to the question of why a person has joined the Zionist Church is: 'I was ill. They prayed for me. Now I am well.' In the same way in West Africa, the purification rites of the Independent Churches are associated with healing. The West African Water Healing Society has features which are reminiscent of pagan practices by which sick persons were cleansed from evil spirits. Here we see again how African thought does not separate as we do the external and the internal, sickness and evil, forgiveness and healing. Water, particularly running water, will be used in a religious service, as a symbol and instrument of washing away sins just as the confession of sins acts as a medical cure, 'an elimination of evil matter in the patient's body'.[4] There is something intensely pathetic in the fact that healing seems to be the main element in the work of many such Churches in South Africa, for, as

[1] Welbourn, op. cit. Pp. 42, 192.
[2] Parrinder, op. cit. P. 118.
[3] Sundkler, op. cit. P. 220.
[4] Sundkler, op. cit. P. 211.

Sundkler says, the real clue to an understanding of the appeal of the healing message . . . is to be found in the social setting where ill-health, malnutrition and child mortality take a terrible toll.

Whatever superstition or folly there may be in this rejection of medicine, the emphasis of the Independent Church should draw attention to the failure of Western civilisation and the failure of Western Christianity to baptise medicine into Christ. Africans recognise what we often deny, that man is a unity, a spirit-body in which or in whom health and wholeness, physical, mental and spiritual, though they are distinguishable in thought, are yet inseparable in fact. Africans see all too often that Western medicine, though it is practised in mission hospitals, works with a mechanistic view of the body. Africans recognise and appreciate the mission doctor who calls nurses, patients and relatives to pray before an operation, but Western doctors and hospitals give the impression all too often that religion has nothing to do with medicine. African thinking, unless it has been twisted and split by contact with Europeans, always looks for a spiritual cause and a spiritual cure for disease. Here surely the African is nearer to the Biblical view of man and health and sickness. 'When Jesus saw their faith, he said to the paralysed man, "My son, your sins are forgiven." Now there were some lawyers sitting there and they thought to themselves "Why does the fellow talk like that? This is blasphemy! Who but God alone can forgive sins?" Jesus knew in his own mind that this was what they were thinking, and said to them: "Why do you harbour thoughts like these? Is it easier to say to this paralysed man, 'Your sins are forgiven', or to say, 'Stand up, take your bed and walk'? But to convince you that the Son of Man has the right on earth to forgive sins"—he turned to the paralysed man—"I say to you, stand up, take your bed and, go home." And he got up, took his stretcher at once, and went out in full view of them all.' [1]

At another point in the proclamation of the Gospel of the Kingdom the Independent Churches give a necessary emphasis. They take witchcraft seriously. Evidence from all parts of Africa shows that in recent years there has been a reappearance or a recrudescence of witchcraft. A report from Central Africa speaks of belief in the power of witchcraft as well-nigh universal. In illness the diviner is called in to name the person who caused the trouble. From West Africa it is reported that the common explanation of suffering and death connects them with witchcraft. Last year the Synod of Livingstonia of the Church of Central Africa Presbyterian was greatly concerned because of the activities of a certain exorcist, Chikanga. Thousands of men and women travelled from great distances to be cleansed by him of witchcraft. Pressure had been put on Church members to attend and many had done so. Africans who did not go along with the others were suspected of having something to hide. It was far easier to do what others were doing, to make confession and so to be cleansed. The ceremony of purification had incorporated some Christian hymns in which the praises of Chikanga were sung. The Synod had called on its members to stand fast, to examine themselves and their presentation of the Gospel. If, they said, we are truly preaching the Saviourhood of Jesus Christ 'why do so many seek salvation from their sins in magicians such as Chikanga'? [2]

It is largely because of the African belief in witchcraft and its link with the Biblical teaching about demons that the Independent Churches in other parts of Africa have gained such

[1] Mark 2, 5-12. (New English Bible.)
[2] Foreign Mission Report. General Assembly of the Church of Scotland, 1961.

strength in numbers and influence. When there was a revival
of witchcraft in Ghana a few years ago under the name of
Tigare, many Christians were excluded from the mission
Churches because of their adherence to the cult. When Tigare
was later exposed as a fraud the disciplined Christians for the
most part joined Independent Churches like the Musama Dis-
co Christi Church. They still believed in the evil spirit who
had stolen his power from God. When they joined the Independent Church they made their confession and 'vomited'
Tigare exactly as the detainees in the Kenya prison camps
were said to 'vomit' Mau Mau. Dr. Parrinder describes how
Christians of the Independent Churches in Nigeria wear magi-
cal charms, amulets, bracelets and anklets to ward off evil
spirits.[1]

The extraordinary case of Alice Lenshina Mulenga and the
rise of the Lumpa Church in Northern Rhodesia since 1954 is
a remarkable proof of the power of the old ideas of magic and
witchcraft among Christians as well as non-Christians. Alice
Lenshina, a Christian of some years standing, belonging to a
village in the Chinsali district, claimed that she had come back
from the dead. She told of her visions and of her call to preach.
Soon the church in Lubwa was too small for the people who
came to hear her. Her fame spread far and wide in Central
Africa. In the dry season of 1956, up to 1,000 pilgrims came in
a week to her village.[2] Her message to begin with was apparently the simple evangelical message that she had been taught
as a catechumen but soon she started to baptise people, telling
them, 'Bring your magic horns and charms, then you will be
saved in God's judgment'. Thousands of Christians came to
be baptised by her a second time, half of whom had been at-

[1] Parrinder, op. cit. P. 159 f.
[2] Taylor and Lehmann: *Christians of the Copperbelt.* P. 250.

tached to Roman Catholic mission churches.[1] The District Commissioner at Chinsali interviewed Alice and warned her that she would not get Government permission to establish her own Church. But it was clear that she could not be charged with offences under the Witchcraft Ordinance. She had no need to point out or accuse anybody of witchcraft because crowds of people came to her spontaneously, bringing their magic 'medicines' and charms with them, leaving these with her and making confession of their sins in order to be cleansed. Her message of deliverance for those who surrendered their magic objects was far more powerful than the efforts of the orthodox Churches. As a District Officer wrote in 1955, 'The extent of her following—60,000 pilgrims to her village in one year—is an indication of how unsatisfying the modern missionary approach to witchcraft is for the majority of Africans. Lenshina does not say that witchcraft is nonsense but that she has been given the power to neutralise it.' [2]

It is all too easy to dismiss the Independent Churches and their creeds as an amalgam of Christianity and animism or, as the late E. W. Smith, author of *The Golden Stool*, more properly described it, dynamism, the belief in an energy immanent in all things, a power that can work equally for good or ill. Sundkler has described the Zionist and Ethiopian Churches in South Africa as bridges over which Africans are brought back to heathenism. But he also quotes Dr. Audrey Richards who, from an intimate study of the tribes in Northern Rhodesia, says that the result of white contact is in many instances an actual increase in the dread of witchcraft and therefore in the whole incidence of magic throughout the group.[3] Magic, he adds, does not give way to modernism but is only driven

[1] Taylor and Lehmann, op. cit. P. 261.
[2] Taylor and Lehmann, op. cit. P. 266.
[3] Sundkler, op. cit. P. 261.

underground. The Church's wisdom would seem therefore to demand a deeper effort to understand this hidden but powerful factor. The Rev. Vernon Stone claims that 'the deepest powers and influences in the life of practically all Africans, Christians included, are the still unbaptised demonic powers that work through witchcraft and magic'. This is true, he says, even of Christian leaders of long standing. He goes on to argue that the missionary is at a disadvantage because he confronts the power of the spirit world with an attitude of unbelief. The African pastor, on the other hand, is aware of its prevalence and power.[1] So also Sundkler says that the Zionist prophet 'shares to the full with his Zionist followers and his pagan friends their dread of witchcraft and their belief in its terrible reality'.[2]

Having considered various aspects of the meeting of the Christian-Western culture with African thought and life, we must see whether it is possible to draw any conclusions which can be of help in the Church's presentation of the Gospel in contemporary Africa. Perhaps the first thing to note, especially for the Churches which lay the greatest emphasis on the preaching of the Word, is that the Gospel as it is heard need not by any means be the same thing as the Gospel which is proclaimed. What men receive and assimilate depends on their own background and pattern of thought as well as on the personality and message of the preacher and the whole culture which he represents. J. V. Taylor points out, for example, that the Church Missionary Society in Uganda from the first preached Moravian and Anglican evangelical theology in terms of the Fall, the Atonement and the offer of salvation in response to repentance and faith in Christ, and the promise of

[1] Vernon Stone: *Scottish Journal of Theology.* June 1955.
[2] Sundkler, op. cit. P. 261.

the Holy Spirit. Yet the message which became the foundation of the Church was the news of the unknown and scarcely heeded Creator God, whom they called Katonda. This was not (as we would assume) because the message was more apposite or easier to believe. 'The revelation of a transcendent, personal and righteous God was not relevant but revolutionary, to the Baganda, yet that was the Word which they heard. The fact that they did hear it, and did not, at that stage, for the most part, hear the message of the Saviourhood of Christ or the Power of the Spirit, though these were the themes that were being preached, suggests that this was the Word of God to them and it was independent of the word of the preacher.'[1]

This report from Uganda connects with Sundkler's suggestion that one of the two foci of the theological encounter in Africa is the doctrine of Creation. This aspect of the Biblical message which is scarcely perceptible in our Western Churches is most prominent in Bantu preaching. Referring to a sermon on the Resurrection chapter, Ezekiel 37, Sundkler says, '(the preacher) began where all Zulu sermons begin, in the Beginning. In the Beginning God created heaven and earth and the sea and the animals—and man.'[2] So the preacher went over the Biblical history from Adam to Christ, finishing with the Resurrection when the Second Adam gained the victory and the First Adam had peace. This Zulu preacher illustrated a very noticeable feature of African Christian thought and preaching, its intense interest in the Old Testament. The resemblance between many of the Bible stories and African myths has also been noted by various scholars. African Christians have a strong feeling of affinity with the People of God in the Old Testament. They recognise their own history in it. Therefore

[1] Taylor: *The Growth of the Church in Buganda.* P. 253.

[2] Sundkler: *The Christian Ministry in Africa.* Swedish Institute of Missionary Research. Uppsala. 1960 P. 283.

the Christian theology which is most likely to carry conviction with them will be a theology which links the natural and the supernatural, Adam and Christ, God and the elementary facts of birth and growth, life and death.

Sundkler's other focus for the theological encounter in Africa is the People of God and the clan community of the Living and the Dead. Those familiar with African traditional thought have often remarked that popular sentiment is often centred in clan-loyalties and clan-conceptions long after Western culture has made an apparently decisive impact on the people. The deep emotional significance of land-use and inheritance, for instance, is wrapped up in the idea that the clan-community includes the 'dead' as well as the living and that it is held in trust for those yet to be born. The clan is the link between the past, the present and the future and as such has a particular resistance and persistence. 'The national gods, requiring public temples, could be destroyed by the Christian oligarchy. But the clan gods, incarnate in rocks and trees and swarms of bees, were much more viable and still persist.' [1] How much more, then, the ancestors have to be reckoned with.

We are not surprised that in different parts of Africa, funeral rites are a problem for the Christian Church. Dr. Baeta of the University of Ghana has summarised the problem: 'For whatever others may do in their own countries, our people *live* with their dead. This is plain for anybody to see who participates sympathetically in a ceremony of the pouring of family libations; the intimate and affectionate tone of the prayers, the sense of the immediate presence of the dead, all that can leave no one in any doubt. And yet when Church bodies make rulings in the matter of funeral observances the reasons given for

[1] Welbourn, op. cit. P. 29.

the repressive measures recommended—are not even religious reasons. . . . The better way of dealing with such-like intractable remains of a previous or passing culture, no longer desired, would seem to be not to proscribe them out of hand but to prune, purify and guide them, making them fit for new and higher service.'[1] We should therefore expect Christian theology in Africa to place more emphasis on the Communion of Saints, on the Church as the great Family of the Living and the 'Dead'.

A Zulu student (Lutheran) in an essay on the subject 'Why and how I became a student of theology' takes the question of the fate of the dead as the central point for a study of the missionary approach. The following extract from this essay is quoted by Sundkler: 'The missionaries came with Christianity but missed the open gate for Christianisation. The message was not applied to the existing forms of worship. They brought good news for mankind, containing forgiveness of sins by Christ alone, who died for all and went to the dead to show them who He was and came up from the dead to show himself to the living ones. As the missionaries preached this Christ, they missed the gate. How was it missed? The missionaries did not show the Africans that they were a considerable nation by respecting their ways of worship and the belief they had; they did not encourage them and tell them that the Bible itself says that the deceased are not dead but are living or resting, and that their spirits were living because they belonged to God from whom they came by the creation of Adam. . . . Our first missionaries missed the gate. They would have won many people by transforming the old belief into the new and by changing the way of approaching the Almighty. The deceased

[1] C. G. Baeta: *Christianity and African Culture*. Christian Council, Gold Coast. 1955. P. 59.

could have been compared with the angels of God which are never worshipped but just praised as God's messengers. Something must be done to establish contact between the old belief and Christianity. Connect both—there is the key to enter the African door and the African's heart.'[1] This use of the doctrine of the Creed, the Descensus ad Inferos, as referring primarily to the dead, will no doubt be questioned. According to Dr. Selwyn in his essay on 1 Peter iii. 18-iv. 6,[2] the reference in this and related passages in the New Testament is primarily to the overthrow of the Satanic powers and not to the liberation of the Righteous Dead. Yet we cannot doubt that this use of the descent into Sheol in African preaching to refer to the dead is legitimate. It proclaims again the theology of the Second Adam declared Son of God by a mighty act in that he rose from the dead. The Risen Christ is the life-giving Spirit. He is Himself the link between the living and the dead. 'This is why Christ died and came to life again, to establish his lordship over dead and living.'[3]

A third point of emphasis for the theology of the African Church arises naturally from our previous discussion of the power of witchcraft and the belief in evil spirits which persists to this day in Africa. From this we would infer that the Gospel which is to prove the power of God for the salvation of Africans is likely to be much nearer the classic idea of the Atonement than the individualistic pietistic gospel of private religion. Perhaps Africans do not have a strongly developed sense of sin as understood in the Evangelical Movement. On the other hand they may be better able to appreciate the idea of the Atonement as the divine conflict and triumph—the story of Christus Victor—as set forth in the Gospels. Recent theologi-

[1] Sundkler, op. cit. P. 290 f.
[2] E. G. Selwyn: *The First Epistle of St Peter*. Macmillan. 1949. PP. 314-362.
[3] Romans 14, 9. (New English Bible.)

cal writing in the West has made some mention of the demonic powers which threaten to rule and destroy man's life but, compared with the Jews in Christ's time or Africans today, the thought of the principalities and powers, the world rulers of darkness, is hardly taken seriously. It is too dramatic for common sense. Yet this is precisely the setting of the Christian story of our redemption, telling how the strong Son of God won the victory over sin and death, how He assumed His royal power and reigns now till all His enemies are made His footstool. T. R. Glover, after describing the Jewish conception of the spirit world at war with God, continues: 'into that war . . . came a new force—the Son of God, the Lord of Glory. He battled with the powers of evil and the battle went strangely and they trapped him. They crucified the Lord of Glory and inflicted on God the most awful disaster that could be conceived. Then it turned out that so far from defeating God's purposes, they had only played into the hands of God. For the defeat of Christ on the Cross led to the Resurrection, to the triumph of God over the demon powers, to captor made captive, death conquered, mankind set free; and all the glorious promises of spiritual liberty and of peace with God which the Christian world knows, and in which it rejoices '.[1]

One can readily see that this is the preaching of the Cross and Resurrection which is addressed to the soul of Africa with its haunting sense of the evil powers which cause sin and calamity and death. This work of Christ on the heroic scale, God breaking into history with the powers of another world, advancing, in the words of Dibelius, 'into enemy-occupied territory', goes on until even the principalities and powers come to understand and to accept God's redemptive purpose. (Colossians 1, 20; Ephesians 3, 10.) It is this theology, arising di-

[1] T. R. Glover: *Jesus in the Experience of Men.* S.C.M. Press. 1921. P. 3.

rectly from the New Testament, which fits the need of Africa more than the traditional outlook of our own modern individualism in religion or in life. 'If in India Jesus Christ, the Guru, may appear as the Truth who saves from the unreality of the world of phenomena, so in Africa the same Christ, the King, proves Himself to be the Life and the Fullness with power to liberate from sickness and death and the devil.' [1] Here again we see, as in the case of belief in magic or witchcraft, that it is foolish and harmful to dismiss the African's fears of the evil agency behind natural phenomena. When African society can be disordered by such a belief, when the established Churches can be so weakened by it, when new Independent Churches can thrive largely on their claims to deal with it, we ought to try to enter into the world of African thought and life where this thing is a terrible reality. As Professor Alan Richardson says, we do not advance our understanding of 'demons' by using scientific jargon like inhibitions, complexes, schizophrenia, paranoia and so on. 'A more genuinely scientific approach might accept devil-possession as, in the circumstances, a legitimate therapeutic hypothesis; but the attitude of one Government servant is rare: "I am a Christian doctor; and Christ has power over devils".' [2]

If we turn to the positive elements in Western culture to which Africans are now heirs through the spread of education and the activities of the Welfare State, it is equally important to interpret these in terms of our Christian faith. We of the West find it very easy to warn Asia and Africa against the cares of the world and the false glamour of riches while at the same time we continue to raise our standard of living by making greater use of applied science to improve our health, to

[1] Sundkler: *The Christian Ministry in Africa.* Swedish Institute of Missionary Research, Uppsala. 1960. P. 281.
[2] Welbourn, op. cit. P. 239, Note 7.

increase our production and to enhance our comfort and leisure. Since, in spite of our frequent disappointment with the achievements of civilised living, we still give so much attention to education and economics, politics and the social services, it would be more consistent for us to share our faith as well as our criticism with our fellows in other lands. This is the point at which it becomes important to see clearly where we stand as Christians in regard to the material world and the conditions of human life in the here and now.

If we regard the world as the God-given sphere of man's experience and education, even if it be only a probationary training exercise with a view to a fuller life beyond, then we need not apologise for taking the world seriously. The good things of life are then good whether they are material or spiritual because they are derived from the Father of lights. They come *from above* though they are ours through man's increasing knowledge of and co-operation with the laws of the physical universe. We can and we must claim that in the fight against poverty and malnutrition and disease, waged by scientific methods, as in the struggle for simplicity and integrity and unselfishness in public life, the battle is not ours but God's. He has given us our environment in nature and society to be a school of manhood, and the making of a better world (though men have spoken of it with such folly and vanity) is still part of our practical training. Though our true home lies beyond, it is in the dust and heat of this world, with its material as well as its spiritual difficulties and problems that we have to discharge our responsibilities as the sons of God. If we believe with Dr. Denney that 'the universe is a system of things in which good can be planted and in which it can bear fruit; that it is also a system of things in which there is a ceaseless and unrelenting reaction against evil',[1] then we are bound to

[1] James Denney: *The Christian Doctrine of Reconciliation.* P. 201 f.

claim for Christ every effort that man makes to co-operate with nature for the enhancement of man's freedom and health and joy.

Professor Macmurray claims that science is not only the product of Christianity but its most adequate expression.[1] Christian evangelism as well as Christian faith has suffered immeasurable loss because theology has failed to show that Christ is the Lord of all good life and that this includes the good life won for us by science as well as the beauty of the natural world and the love of home and friends. We have seen the part that Christian education can play in interpreting to young Africans the heritage of Western knowledge and skill. The efforts of Christian missions in the past have linked medical care and healing with the revelation of God's love for men. Agricultural development and social welfare have also featured in the missionary programme. It is obvious, of course, that the Church as an official body cannot keep pace with Africa's expanding need for outside help. Christians, however, engaged in every form of scientific and humanitarian service can do what no Church as such can do. Nothing can be more vital at this stage in Africa than a true, balanced Christian witness through the medium of material and physical help. 'If we are to meet the tremendous challenge of secular civilisation with its claim that man with the aid of science can accomplish by his own efforts all and more than all, than any God has done for his worshippers, we must bring to the peoples of Asia and Africa in Christ's name and as God's gift the best that secular civilisation has to offer, knowing all the time that in itself it is nothing.' [2]

We must return, however, to consider how the Gospel may be presented to Africans over against the Bantu world-view.

[1] John Macmurray: *The Clue to History*. P. 86.
[2] J. H. Oldham. An address delivered to the Conference of Missionary Societies on 'Rethinking Missions'.

As we saw in considering Christianity and Politics, Africans do not distinguish, as we unconsciously do, between religion and life. It is only the more sophisticated who divide life into compartments labelled sacred or secular, economic, political, religious and so on. So African Christianity, too, strikes us as utilitarian and materialistic. The Church itself is judged by its usefulness as a social institution and Africans take for granted that the Church, when it is true to its Gospel, will be on the side of their political advancement. In spite of the rising tide of materialism in the modern Western sense which can be seen everywhere in Africa, the old framework of African thought persists and must be understood if the Gospel is to be proclaimed to Africa's need and condition. 'The Bantu worldview', say the authors of *Christians of the Copperbelt*, 'appears to contain no distinction between a natural and a supernatural order of being; even among those Africans who have adopted Western categories of thought, there are many who cannot fully accept the divorce between heaven and earth. Christian teaching, it is true, brought into greater prominence the old idea of the great God who is above and beyond all; and with this had appeared the imagery of a heavenly country which is "somewhere else". But these concepts have not greatly modified the belief that Nature, Man and the Unseen are inseparably involved in one another in a total community of which it might be said that all is here and all is now. A man's wellbeing consists in his belonging to and being in harmony with, this totality.' [1]

We saw, at a previous step in our discussion, that in Uganda the preaching of the Gospel of evangelical Christianity, though it laid its emphasis on the Saviourhood of Christ, was heard as the good news of the Creator God who had a name in every

[1] Taylor and Lehmann: *Christians of the Copperbelt.* P. 275 f.

part of Africa but whose character was unknown and whose existence was thought of as too remote and beyond the world for him to have any dealings now with men or they with him. This suggests that the way for the Gospel to enter more fully into the African mind would be by a greater emphasis on the unity of God the Father and God the Son, and the cosmic redemption that Christ has accomplished. 'The worst heresy, next to that of dividing religion and righteousness', said George Macdonald, 'is to divide the Father from the Son and to represent the Son as doing that which the Father does not Himself do.' That is the weakness of all theories of the Atonement which lay the main stress on the sacrifice made by Christ to God on man's behalf and Christ's offer of individual salvation.

If we take our stand on the New Testament assertion that God was in Christ reconciling the world to himself, emphasising both the presence and action of the transcendent God in Christ and the fact that the object of his action was the *world*, then we leave the way open to show that the relation of God transcendent to the world, and the condition of the world itself has been changed by what Christ did on the Cross. 'No object is sufficient for the love of God short of the world itself . . . it is a sin of the world that Christ takes away.' [1] Over against the African feeling that Nature, Man and the Unseen are involved in one another we set the Gospel of the Unity of God and the reconciliation of the world and man in God. Moreover the Christian Saviour is one with the Christ through whom and for whom the universe was created. In Him, says Paul, the universe holds together. He who became man for us men and for our salvation has not left the world or us as orphans in the world. The categories of space and time do not restrict the Ascended Lord or quench the Holy Spirit.

[1] Wm. Temple on John 3, 16. (*Readings in St. John's Gospel.*)

He who ascended is here because 'the right hand of God is here in the life of man in history, and this is where the Word may be encountered'.[1] There is no need to scale the heavens to find Him for He is among us. The gulf between God and man has been closed by Him who is the Head and King of our race, who has united us to Himself and to one another in the Holy Spirit who is the bond of our fellowship and purpose in Him.

Thus the argument seems to bring us back to the fundamental Christian doctrine of the Unity of God. We seldom hear this preached in our Churches. A special effort is made on Trinity Sunday but this truth is either too difficult for our people or it is not felt to need any emphasis. Yet the recovery of this note is a real Gospel to the world today and nowhere more than in Africa. 'Hear, O Israel, the Lord our God, the Lord is One' (Deuteronomy 6, 4) is a message of hope and deliverance. The Unity of God is the basis for a re-integration of Christian faith and wholeness of living. Dr. Warren points to this urgency in the case of educated Africans. The dilemma of young Africans is to bridge the gulf between their Christian schooling and life: 'To them God is the God of the Church. He is not the God of politics and social life. They need help to see Him as one God: to see that the Church is concerned with the whole of life. . . . To see Him as *one* God—the *One*—is the supreme need of our time, the peculiar saving content of the Gospel in this disintegrated generation which only knows unity as something it has not got.' [2]

The Christian Churches and missions from the West need to possess this basic insight if they are to bring the fullness of the Gospel to Africa. The Church in Africa too needs this

[1] R. Gregor Smith: *The New Man.* S.C.M. Press. 1956. P. 47 f.
[2] Max Warren: *The Christian Mission.* S.C.M. Press. 1951. P. 9 f.

vision if it is to enter into closer, more creative and redemptive contact with the revolutionary forces which are changing African society. It is needed for a fully integrated Christian education, and for the proper witness of the Christian layman in secular life. The Gospel of the Unity of God is the spring of Christian action in politics and race relations. It brings the fire of an evangelical experience into the community and all its affairs. From a deep sense of God's omnipresence it treats the common life as sacred. This is the prophetic attitude which, in Oman's words, reveals itself in the right secularising of religion. This is the true monotheism crowned by Jesus Himself 'because it neither identifies anything with God nor separates anything from His meaning and purpose'.[1]

[1] John Oman: *The Natural and the Supernatural*. Cambridge. 1931. P. 469.

MISSIONARY PARTNERS IN A
NEW PATTERN

Two phrases used in the previous lecture give us a good
guide to round off our discussion of the Christian task in
Africa as we see it today. The first is the Unity of God and the
second the right secularising of religion. We must try to see
Africa not from a Western colonial point of view nor even
from a Western Christian's point of view—as a field for Christian missions. We must first seek to see what God is doing in
Africa. This leaves room, of course, for the Christian mission,
but it affords a breadth and scope for all the forces impinging
on the life of Africa: economic, educational, political; the
United Nations, the various groupings of the new independent States of Africa, the relation between India and Africa,
Islam in Africa, and so on. Nor can we afford to forget the
influence of African participation in movements outside Africa.
It is a sign of the times that the African group in the United
Nations is expected soon to number thirty,[1] and they will be
the largest group in the Assembly, nearly equal in numbers to
the Western Europe, pre-war Commonwealth countries and
the Soviet bloc combined. It is perhaps equally significant
that, whereas the Christian Church has by and large regarded
North Africa, from Egypt to Morocco, as belonging more to
Europe and the Mediterranean than to Africa, the new President of the United Nations, Mr. Mongi Slim of Tunisia, is
hailed as the man from Africa. However we estimate the rela-

---

[1] *Note.* According to the latest information (November 1962) the total membership of the United Nations is now 110, of which 32 are African States.

tive importance of these many factors of change making for cohesion or conflict—the Portuguese in Angola, internal convulsions in the Congo, clashes between Europeans and Africans in Central Africa, the strife of K.A.D.U. and K.A.N.U. in Kenya, the problem of Buganda in Uganda, and the almost universal bitter reaction to South African apartheid throughout the rest of Africa—one thing is clear, that Africa and African history is being made in our time.

Can we not say humbly and confidently that God has committed to man an Africa that is still uncreated? When we think of the deep and profound differences within Africa, of the ending of the colonial era and the beginning of a new era of international relations spot-lighting Africa and linking Africa as never before with the rest of the world, we must recognise that Africa both is and is not a reality. It is still in process of becoming. What it will be depends on what the races of men make of it, for God in His wise providence has set men on the face of Africa, and set Africa before men, not simply as a problem for their intelligence and a test of their character but as the medium of their co-operation with each other and the means of their fellowship with Him. God has control of events in Africa. He controls its history with a view to the education and growth of His children towards a maturity which will enable them to enter into His gracious purposes, and that means that they can use the material environment, and accept the challenge of the social and political opportunity as it varies from place to place and from time to time, to do God's will and to seek His Kingdom throughout the whole range of their experience. We claim that, as Christians, we can to some extent understand what God is doing in Africa in our time because God is working His purpose out (and we know what that purpose is through Christ) and He speaks to men through events and through the world for He is over all and through all and in all, the one God and Father of all. This is God's work in the world and so it is God's work in Africa. So, before we seek to distinguish the work of the Church as such or try to evaluate the policies or methods used in the mission of the Church, we must first get the right angle of vision, that is, we must begin with the unity of God and the universality of His Kingdom.

This trinity of God, man and the world or, to use the title of Archbishop Temple's Gifford Lectures, *Nature, Man and God*, gives us a different approach to the Church's mission in Africa from what has been familiar in recent years. Since the International Missionary Council met at Tambaram, Madras, in 1938, all the emphasis has been placed on the Church, and this was necessary because a distinction had grown up between 'the mission' or missions and the Church, which made *mission* an optional extra for Christians, concealed the nature of the Church itself and demoted the so-called Younger Churches to the status of poor relations of 'missions'. Hence the titles of the Tambaram and Willingen Conferences, 'The World Mission of the Church' and 'The Missionary Obligation of the Church', represented a much-needed correction and emphasis, and it is largely due to this swing of the pendulum that the World Council of Churches and the International Missionary Council, both springing out of the World Missionary Conference of Edinburgh, 1910, have been able to unite. During the last fifty years, we may say, there has been a steady growth in the missionary consciousness of the Churches parallel with the church-consciousness of the missions of which we have been speaking. It is this mutual drawing-together which leads us to believe that the aim of this union, as stated in the Constitution of the integrated Council, in its Commission on World Mission and Evangelism, will be powerfully advanced, that is, 'to further the proclamation to the whole world of the Gospel of Jesus Christ to the end that all men may believe in Him and be saved'.

Unfortunately, as I think, this much-needed concentration on the Church coincided with a movement in theology away from the world. By that I mean the too exclusive concern with the Church as our objective—we might also say God's objective—rather than the world for whose salvation Christ gave Himself and for whose sake His Church is called to suffer and serve. No doubt the theology with which the Christian students of the First World War and its aftermath were strongly imbued was often too optimistic, even superficial. But it had the merit of taking the Kingdom of God as its starting point and so it could not overlook social duty and corporate righteousness, even when most concerned for personal conversion. However the strong reaction against this approach, largely influenced by German missionary thinking, gave a strong negative emphasis to our conception of economics and politics. I remember that, at the Tambaram Meeting of the International Missionary Council, the report of the Section on The Church and the Changing Social and Economic Order had to be rewritten three times because of the acute difference of opinion on the point of whether the Kingdom of God could ever have any reference to the existing social order except condemnation and judgment. At times the attitude of resignation, or acceptance of things as they were, was expressed so bluntly that it drew forth the caricature of the hymn 'Rise up, O men of God', one verse of which reads:

> 'Sit down, O men of God,
> His Kingdom He will bring,
> Whenever it may please His Will,
> You cannot do a thing.'

But the negative theology of that period, while it did not lead to a diminution of missionary effort, did weaken the conviction with which much of our work was done. If I am not mistaken it led to a loss of the deeper sanctions for much of the educational, social and medical effort which had been and is still characteristic of the best missionary effort. Coupled with the new concentration on the Church and its life and growth, this tended to the isolation of the Church, the separation of religion from life and the reduction of medical and educational missions to the level of a social service.

These considerations suggest that we have reached a point in the Christian understanding of mission where we have to make a new effort to do justice both to the Church and to the world so that we recognise fully the Lordship of Christ over World *and* Church. However this immense and difficult theme is to be handled, it would seem as if no other was so determinative of the practical problem which, after all, lies at the root of all missionary theology, that is the right relation of the Church to the world. What we must conserve is the fundamental confession of Christian faith that Christ is the World's Redeemer and Lord. All theology, it has been said, is primarily an effort to state the relation of God to the world. Dr. Kraemer, in *The Christian Message in a non-Christian World*,[1] makes this emphasis again and again. All the debates on Christianity and Science, Christianity and Culture, the Social Gospel, Education and Evangelism, etc., stem from different interpretations of this foundation-truth. If that is so, however much we love the Church, however we think of the Church as the Body of Christ, the Household of faith, the Apostle to the nations, we must not allow the Church to get in the way so as to obscure the Kingdom which is both in the world and

[1] Edinburgh House Press. 1938.

above the world, both in time and eternity. Certainly God works in and through the Church to proclaim His Gospel and reveal His will but is it not as important and perhaps more encouraging, as we look at the state of the Church, to remember that God also works beyond and above us, that His ways are not our ways or the ways of our Churches, and that it is the world and not the Church which is His primary concern? Dr. John Baillie, preaching the closing sermon of the Student Christian Congress in St. Giles' Cathedral in 1958, chose John 3, 16 as his text, 'God so loved the world. . . .' In the course of his sermon, he said, 'It was because God loved what He had in mind to make that He first made it; and now He continues to love it because He made it that it might be loved'. To say 'I believe in God the Father Almighty, Maker of Heaven and Earth' as in the Apostles' Creed, is to say 'The world is in the hands of the living God, whose will for it is wholly good'. In the world of our time with its apparently infinite possibilities for scientific advance, its balance of terror, its exploration of space, its contrast between poverty and plenty, and its unity for good or ill, the primitive Christian confession, Jesus Christ is Lord, is the most daring and the most difficult affirmation we can make.

The proclamation of this Gospel, Jesus Christ is Lord, was possible because of the Resurrection, and that great Fact, though it could not be witnessed and attested in the way that the normal occurrences of every day can be seen and described, was yet a secular event, an event in the world in which we live, an event which belongs to all human history. So it is to-day. To proclaim Christ as Lord is to say that He is Lord of the revolutions in Africa and that He is at the centre of African history now. Whether we see His mercy or His judgment in the blend of apparent good and evil, in the upsurge of life among backward peoples, or the clash of party in the new States of Africa, or the confusion of interested and disinterested help offered from outside to emerging African nations, this one assertion Christian faith requires—that God is working His purpose out by the power of Christ's life and death and resurrection, that His purpose concerns the whole life of Africa and that this means for the Christian, life in the world and for the world.

Yet the Church in Africa is obviously the pivot of the Christian mission to Africa. The Church as the family of God, Christ's members gathered in little communities in every part of the continent, in the villages, on the mining compounds, in the African townships, wherever they are, *they* are Christ's witnesses, strange and incredible as it may seem. As the little flock of the Good Shepherd, as the disciples called to be with their Master and sent out by Him into the world at their own doors, they are the light of that world, they are the salt of the earth for Africa. The fellowship of forgiven sinners, very backward, often only semi-literate, still struggling against ancient powers of evil as well as modern idolatries, they constitute the Church of the Lord Jesus, the King. Of course the fellowship also includes professional men, doctors, teachers, politicians, lawyers, and they may be and often are, active in church as well as society, but they are no more and no less the people of God than the great under-privileged majority of their neighbours. It is in these communities and through them that the Holy Spirit is working. The Church of God in this place, or that, whether well-known or obscure, progressive or backward, relatively prosperous or very poor, is the minister, the servant of Christ, *there* in its community, and no foreign mission or agency from outside can do its work, or take its place. This group of baptised Christians is the representative of Christ and of the Church in all the world to that particular community.

Only in our day can we speak without entire exaggeration of the Church of Africa. Divided as it is by race and colour in certain areas and divided everywhere by the denominational bias introduced with the Churches and missions of the West, it has yet begun to sense its togetherness as the Church of God in Africa. This comes as the reward and result of the work of Christian councils in different parts of the continent, and of the overall insight and concern of the International Missionary Council. The African Churches showed their eagerness to meet each other and to learn from their brethren in other parts of Africa, most notably at the All-African Church Conference at Ibadan, Nigeria, in 1958. The Conference recorded with 'astonished joy' its sense that Christians were one in Christ, whether white or black, educated or illiterate, indigenous African or adopted African, and it spoke of its anxiety to demonstrate that unity not only in the Church but between tribes and races and nations so that all would see that 'our brother is the Yoruba, the Zulu, the Afrikaner, the Kikuyu, the Englishman, the Indian, the Frenchman and any other person who acknowledges Africa as his home, and gives to it his loyalty and his gifts'.[1] The Provisional Committee of the Conference later appointed Dr. Donald M'Timbulu as its Secretary, and with the help of the World Council of Churches and the International Missionary Council, regional and local consultations have been arranged to bring the Churches closer for mutual encouragement and strengthening. Thus it may well be that the Church in Africa will increasingly draw the

[1] L. B. Greaves: *International Review of Missions.* July 1958.

peoples of Africa together when so many influences are driving them in different directions and setting before them incompatible aims.

We think, then, of the Church in Africa pursuing its missionary task of proclaiming by word and deed, by the character of its fellowship and by its service of its neighbourhood that Christ is in the midst and that He is Lord of all. The environment of the Church is exercising a constant pressure on the Church and the Church, in so far as it is faithful to its Lord's commission, is seeking to penetrate and to permeate that environment. This means that there is no *modus vivendi* between the Church and the world. The Church exists for the glory of God and for the doing of His will in the world. It must therefore offer its Gospel and witness to its Lord, both in encouragement of all the factors in its environment which can be healthy and wholesome in their effects on men and women, and also in opposition to whatever degrades or weakens or deceives men and women. It seeks for the best opportunities for Africans to lead the Christian life and therefore it seeks for the material conditions, the social conditions, the political conditions which can contribute to the fullest development of the African in freedom and fellowship. Similarly it must seek to criticise and to oppose the influences which make the task of converting Africans and the life of Africa more difficult. Here we see the dilemma of the Church in general as we saw it in terms of education.

'If the Church were to cease to interest itself in the economic, social and intellectual advancement of the peoples of Africa and occupy itself mainly with caring for the "souls" of Africans through its evangelistic and pastoral work, a separation would be made between the religious growth of the African and his growth as a human being. The development of his natural powers and the improvement of his earthly existence would come to be regarded as something secular and be set in competition with his spiritual allegiance. The sense of the unity of life, which is so strong in the African, would be sacrificed and the full meaning of the Gospel as having to do with the redemption of man's whole life would be obscured. If, on the other hand, the energies of the Church should become absorbed in humanitarian and cultural tasks, in a multiplicity of activities directed to intellectual and social improvement, the Church would have betrayed its trust. These activities are saved from corruption and emptiness only when there shines on them a light from the eternal world.' [1]

We must not underestimate the immense difficulty of maintaining this bifocal conception of the Church's task and mission in Africa. We know how seldom any Church or congregation can live consistently in accordance with this standard even in a country with a long tradition of Christian culture such as our own. How much more difficult for a Church in Africa to walk this narrow way between self-centredness, introversion, clericalism on the one hand and humanitarianism, activism and secularism on the other. The scope of the Church's task is so much broader in Africa than here in Britain where the State and the community have undertaken most of the social and welfare services required by the modern community. Just because the Church in Africa is so close to the people, just because religion is integrated with the common life to a degree now seldom understood by us, the task in Africa is harder though the reward is closer to its hand. Hence it is vital for Christians in the rest of the world to consider the present pattern. What obstacles does it offer to the

[1] J. H. Oldham and B. D. Gibson: *The Remaking of Man in Africa.* Oxford University Press. 1931. P. 138 f.

total mission of the Church in Africa? What changes are required in this pattern in order that Christians in other lands may best assist the Church in Africa to bear witness in every possible way to the Lordship of Christ over the world and the Church?

Before looking at possible and desirable changes in this pattern of relationships and activity, it may be wise to state the conditions which it is almost essential to observe if such changes are to be made without damage to the distinctive features and merits of the missionary tradition. Here we are not concerned to defend 'missions' against criticisms but to see where they have stood for something precious in our Christian heritage. The first of these features surely is the concern for evangelism, the movement of the Gospel outward to the non-Christian. Though there has been a great deal of emphasis on the life and needs of the Young Churches of Africa and the East, the traditional and central urge of missionary enthusiasm has always looked beyond the Christian community to those who were without, to the people who sat in darkness because the light of the Gospel of the glory of Christ had not illumined their hearts and lives. We might find, in fact, if we took a Gallup poll of the missionary intercessors and givers in all our Churches, that they missed this evangelical note in the discussions of missionary objectives in recent years because of the continual repetition of the emphasis on the Church in Africa and elsewhere. Whether, therefore, we think of the Gospel in terms of the conversion of individuals or as the Lordship of Christ over men in all their relationships or of the Church as the representative of Christ and His agent of mission to the world, in any case we must seek in any modification of the pattern of activity 'to further the proclamation to the whole world of the Gospel of Jesus Christ to the end that all men may believe in Him and be saved'. Our activities and relationships must assist that movement in Africa, through the Church and with the Church but beyond the Church.

In that movement we will seek to provide personal help and reinforcement by sending men and women to work with and for and alongside the Churches in Africa. Here we are in some difficulty about terminology for the word 'missionary' is suspect in some quarters while, in others, strangely enough, it is a coveted word so that secular and business and public bodies regard their best exponents as 'missionaries' with 'missionary' or 'quasi-missionary' zeal. For our purposes it will be better to use the noun 'missionary' to denote 'the agent of the help which one part of the Church sends to another for the discharge of the common missionary task'.[1] If the word is used in this sense it is in every way preferable to the term 'fraternal worker'. There is room for any number of fraternal workers employed by the Churches in Africa or by Christian Councils or by Societies organised for specific purposes to supplement the work of the Churches. The Churches in Africa might wish to adopt many non-ministerial Christians—e.g. doctors, teachers, social workers, business men, etc.—as 'fraternal workers' so that their life and witness might be acknowledged and that they might in the fullest sense share in the fellowship of the local Church. Much more of this association of expatriate Christians with the Church in Africa is needed. But the specific missionary, so far as one can see, will be required for many years and, once we rid ourselves of any colonial or imperial overtones, it will be recognised as an appropriate and acceptable word for a relationship indispensable to the Christian world mission.

[1] Lesslie Newbigin: *One Body, One Gospel, One World*. International Missionary Council. 1958. P. 47.

The missionary in this exact sense is the living bond between one Church and another, the bond in more senses than one because he not only links the two in his person and by his life but he is, to the African Church which he (or she) serves, the token and pledge of the continuity of the commitment of interest and support in that other Church in Asia or Europe or America or Australia, or anywhere else outside Africa which accepts a missionary task in Africa. The East Asia Christian Conference has already removed much of the adventitious offence in this word because it has published the facts of the Asian participation in the world mission of the Church, showing that some two hundred Asian Christians are working outside the borders of their countries. How many of these are missionaries in the exact sense defined above it is difficult to say, but twenty-eight missionaries have been sent by the Churches in India, of whom twelve have been commissioned by the Mar Thoma Church. Eighteen have gone from the United Church of Christ in the Philippines to Thailand, Indonesia, Hawaii, Ethiopia, and other lands. The United Church in Japan has two missionaries working with Japanese and Canadians in Canada. The Burma Baptist Convention has a missionary in Kenya and another in Nigeria. These are illustrations of the fact that the vital thing to preserve is the readiness of Christians in any part of the world to share the ongoing burden of the Church in Africa. This surely is the essential in the missionary movement, not a West to East direction, not a movement from a 'Christendom' no longer in existence, to 'the heathen world' (unless we mean the world at our own doors) but, all the same, a geographical crossing of frontiers from one land to another, the expression of the nature of the Church as an ecumenical and missionary fellowship, everywhere universal as well as local. This, surely, is what Dr. D. T.

Niles is anxious to conserve when he distinguishes evangelism and mission, 'evangelism as crossing the frontier between faith and non-faith but mission as additionally involving the crossing of secular frontiers with the purpose of belonging to the other side for the sake of the Gospel'.[1] The missionary is a man or woman who goes to make another country his own for Christ's sake and to identify himself with the Church in that country and make its mission his vocation.

In the most intimate connection with the missionary as a person, we need to conserve, if possible, under any changes of pattern, the maximum personal link between Christians in the sending Churches and the Churches in Africa which receive them. Dr. Latourette claims that 'the missionary movement of the past century has been the most notable outpouring of life, in the main unselfish, in the service of alien peoples which the world has ever seen'.[2]

An equally astonishing feature of this work, when you come to think of it, is the missionary education carried on in congregations of the sending Churches and among gatherings of missionary society supporters. In the last 150 years many thousands of Christians in this and other lands have learned to think of Africans and their needs quite personally, have been touched by the sufferings of African lepers or the backwardness of children in African villages, have seen pictures of the African Church in action and have learnt to give to and to pray for individuals by name as if they were near friends and neighbours. If the story of this missionary education could be told and we could see in one place even a small selection of the books and magazines, films and slides, exhibitions and plays, which have been produced for this purpose, it would be ack-

---

[1] *World Council of Churches Division of Studies Bulletin.* Vol. VI, No. 2, p. 12.
[2] K. S. Latourette: *Missions Tomorrow.* Harper & Brothers. 1936. P. 15.

nowledged as perhaps the most powerful means of education which the Church or the voluntary societies have yet devised. We all know that the process has had some effects which are not appropriate, at least in our day, a narrowing of concern to specific bits of missionary work, and a kind of possessiveness towards people and places where 'our mission' or 'our missionary' is at work. Certainly such features must now be eliminated. But with any changes of the pattern it must be our concern to maintain and to multiply the contacts between Christians in the sending countries and the Christians who receive help. In the long run we can't know, love and serve Africa in the full Christian sense of these words unless by knowing, loving and serving Africans. Even a Church of England, a Church of Scotland, Baptist, Congregational or Methodist contribution raised by levy or simply as part of a central Church budget, and devoted to an All-Africa Fund, while it might be necessary to relieve distress or provide buildings or train workers, would not be fully effective from a Christian point of view. A smaller sum raised through a thousand local efforts and linking individuals and groups at both ends of the process would be more deeply influential on life and character because it *unites* them in mission and gives them a sense of the unity of mission, wherever they are, as the same 'at home' and 'abroad'.

While these elements in the tradition of missionary education and organisation are, we believe, of permanent value, it is at the same time obvious that some radical changes are needed in the missionary pattern which we have inherited, and they are nowhere more important than in relation to Africa. The purpose of such changes, as we have already emphasised, should be to secure the maximum effort of the world-wide Christian fellowship working with and through the Church in Africa for the glory of God. One obvious barrier to the free movement of help from outside to meet a particular, perhaps critical, situation inside Africa is the dependent status of many African Churches. They have been established as the result of missionary effort reaching them from a particular Church in the West, and that connection, which, from one point of view, is so precious, can become a source of weakness, even perhaps of bondage. On both sides the situation can easily arouse irritation and resentment. In Africa this sensitiveness is accentuated by the hang-over from colonialism, by the association of missionary and missionary funds with political motives, with the paternalism of an era which, in fact, has ended and has been followed by a far more equal and reciprocal relationship between missionary and African. On the sending side there is a mixture of quite worthy and less worthy motives. There is the possessiveness and narrowness to which we have referred but along with this a proper sense of responsibility for the wisest use of funds and personnel. This attitude, however, does not recognise that the African Church has grown up, that it is already a responsible body, with its own constitution and order, its place in the community and its obligation to be the representative of Christ to its country and nation. The only right attitude therefore is to treat that Church as itself the missionary society in that place, the apostle and minister of Christ, the medium He has chosen for His own possession and through which His Spirit invites men and women to join His fellowship.

If that is so, the Church in Africa is hindered rather than helped, its purpose is blunted and its integrity as Christ's missionary denied when gifts of personnel or funds are given 'with strings' or conditions attached. There is room at this point for fresh thought and effort as to how best the process of consultation can be carried forward so that the receiving Church takes the other into its confidence as to how it wishes to use the help given from outside, but the initiative and the decision should be its own, and the other should not seek to lay down conditions but rather to understand, so that the individuals and groups at 'the home base' who support the effort should do so with a conviction that is in no way weakened because the pattern keeps on changing.

Again it is necessary to examine the pattern of relationships if the whole Church is to bring help where it is most needed. At an earlier stage it was necessary that a particular Church or 'field' in Africa should look to a single denomination or a single missionary society for assistance. At the time there was no other possibility. But that is no longer the case in large areas of Africa. Churches in other parts of the world which have not had an interest or opportunity are ready to supplement the help offered by those earlier on the field. Asian Churches, though primarily interested in Asia, have new and close ties with Africa. Churches in Europe in some cases find that the fields with which they were formerly associated in Asia are now closed to them and they are looking for new opportunities in Africa. Hence there are strong reasons for modifying the pattern of unilateral relationships whereby one Church or society outside Africa had a virtual monopoly of interest in a particular Church in Africa. The principle of mission comity implied that a missionary agency had virtually exclusive 'rights' to a particular geographical area. It was good in its day but it is already out of date when the Church of the area wants more assistance than this one agency can offer, and when other auxiliaries are ready to come in. It is at this point that both the denominational and the national character of the help given has to be modified if there is to be a flexibility in keeping with the change of situation.

The origin of the sending agency in the colonial era naturally corresponded in most cases with the nationality of the colonial power. British missions and Churches predominated in British Africa, German missions in German Africa, and so on. Even then there were many exceptions to the rule and the supra-nationality of missions was already implicit in the First World War in the preservation of German missionary property, and by the great undertaking of Orphaned Missions in the Second World War. It was at Whitby, 1947, however, that the International Missionary Council formulated the principle of supra-nationality as involved in the conception of the universal Christian mission. How far, and in what an immense variety of forms, missionary effort has been internationalised is fully demonstrated in the research pamphlet by the Rev. R. K. Orchard.[1] Our concern here is not so much with the freedom of the sending agency to find fresh fields of effort as with the advantage to the receiving Church if it has freedom to enlist and to use help of various kinds from different countries and different Churches. The multi-lateral relationships making up the pattern of Inter-Church Aid have this great advantage that they imperceptibly alter the situation, in which one Church or society gives and another receives, to form an ecumenical pattern in which the Churches of the so-called 'mission fields' are treated as equal partners in all decisions of where and how the united resources of many Churches are to be used. This means that the psychological sensitiveness of the poor relation no longer affects the decision and there is much more likelihood of tapping new resources of generosity at the receiving as well as giving end of the process. It means that the receiving Churches are associated with giving, and the giving Churches with distributing what others than themselves are giving. Both sides are learning to study where and

[1] R. K. Orchard: *Out of Every Nation*. S.C.M. Press. 1959.

how the needs of the total world mission can best be met in a context in which their particular interest in the giving or receiving is subordinated to the larger purpose.

With the same purpose of broadening the base and enlarging the scope of co-operation in the mission of the Church, the pattern of denominational affiliations needs to be modified. Controversy as to the merits or demerits of world confessionalism and how far it can claim to forward the cause of Christian unity may be expected to continue for a long time. We can affirm, however, that to confine the missionary link between Churches in different countries to the denominational channels is no longer possible or desirable. The Churches of Africa, like the Churches of Asia, are ready to move forward into wider unions. Our divisions do not matter to them, because the doctrinal and historical reasons underlying our divisions have little or no meaning for them. The Young Churches can be and have been gravely hampered by the denominational affiliation when grants or personnel have been withdrawn or conditions have been imposed by the outside partner on grounds of Church order. Even where this has not happened, the Church is in fact hindered in its freedom and fellowship with Churches of other denominations on African soil when it has to comply with requirements of its senior partner if it wants to remain in full communion with the Church or Churches from which it sprang.

At this point there is a real danger that the form of the Church or Churches may fail to do justice to the character and claims of the Gospel. We are reminded of the Fundamental Principle of the Missionary Society as set out in the Plan and Constitution of the London Missionary Society in 1796: 'that its design is not to send Presbyterianism, Independency, Episcopacy or any other form of Church Order or Government, about which there may be difference of opinion among serious persons, but the glorious Gospel of the Blessed God, to the heathen; and that it shall be left (as it ought to be left) to the minds of the persons whom God may call into the fellowship of His Son from among them to assume for themselves such form of Church Government as to them shall appear most agreeable to the word of God'. It may be said that a statement such as this simply reflects the situation in England at that time. The Churches were practically devoid of missionary enthusiasm and the missionary societies were founded in protest and with a view to doing what the Churches themselves should have done. On the other hand it is not enough to say that the Fundamental Principle proves that the Church was not taken seriously because the London Missionary Society was founded in the hope that Anglicans, Presbyterians, Methodists and Congregationalists would join together in one society. This aim was not achieved, partly or mainly because afterwards societies were formed in affiliation with Churches and some Churches established their own missionary committees. In our time it has become so clear to us that the Church is primarily the agent of mission that we naturally expect to see the faith and order of the sending Church represented in the young Church which is derived from it. But, if we revert to what was said about the local Church as the Fellowship of the Spirit and the Apostle and Servant of the Gospel to its people, we must agree that, as soon as may be possible, the Church should be encouraged to chose its own form of Order and Government according to the needs of the country and the possibilities of Union, rather than to conform to the pattern of the sending Church.

Meantime, in the regrettable backwardness of the Western Churches in regard to Reunion, there is much more that could be done to modify the denominational pattern of missionary work. The Churches in Africa as in Asia have enlisted the interest and aid of Churches and societies from the West. This has led the Home Boards, as we still call them, to co-operate and to some extent to pool their ideas. Much more is needed along these lines because the policies of the different sending Churches often mean that in different areas within the same Church in Africa there are divergent aims and methods. It is to be hoped that the time will soon come when the Younger Churches will bring their parent Churches closer together, when representatives of all concerned will meet, preferably 'on the Field', to consult together how best to unite their resources according to the desires and needs of the Church on the spot. It is clear that there is a big and essential task for regional organisations, specially for Christian Councils to see how all the available resources from outside the area can best be used to supplement and to accompany the efforts of the Church, but it is much to be desired that United Boards of Mission in the sending countries may soon be set up to work with and for the new United Churches. This would be the best form of expression in our day of the Fundamental Principle so nobly stated by the London Missionary Society in 1796.

Still looking to the fulfilment of the missionary motive with the greatest flexibility and freedom, we need to examine the programme of work for which missionary bodies have made themselves responsible. It has been a matter of deep concern to many that the greater part of the personnel and funds made available for mission is exhausted in the ongoing life of the Younger Churches so that there is no room for manoeuvre, no resources for advance, no mobility in the character of the mission. It is 'bogged down' in the support of the Church.

When the situation is examined more closely it will be found that much of the effort and expenditure goes to pay for work which goes far beyond the needs of the Christian community in schools, hospitals and welfare services. These so-called 'service' activities have been undertaken by the missionary agency in a variety of circumstances because they were felt to be necessary in a backward community where there was no Government or other provision for them. Moreover, they were felt to be consistent with, if not essential to, the proclamation of the Gospel and the establishment of the Church. The position in regard to such services today has been altered because of changes occurring at both ends of the line of communication. Sometimes the African Government is able to provide the services required. In other cases there is still room for the voluntary agency in schools and hospitals but Government exercises supervision, if not control, and may pay more or less of the cost. Often the cost mounts at a greater rate than the Government grant. Again there are new possibilities in the sending countries because large resources, untouched by missionary agencies, are subscribed for service purposes under the World Council of Churches Inter-Church Aid Department.

It seems then that there is a strong case for the study of how such Inter-Church Aid could help to share the burden of the service activities of the missionary agency. If this is to be done it is important to assert that this division of labour is not due to a division of conviction or opinion between evangelism and service, between a higher and a lower dedication or vocation. The proclamation of the Lordship of Christ needs both words and deeds. The glory of Christ who took upon Himself the form of a servant is revealed today as always by acts of love in the fellowship and beyond the fellowship. The missionary agency of the Church must at all times retain many visible and tangible forms of service to men in their physical and social need. But, by enlisting new sources of support for the vast enterprises of education and medical assistance, freedom from hunger, war on want, etc., in Africa and by bringing them into the closest co-operation with the Church's missionary concerns, it should be possible for some larger proportion of missionaries and mission funds to be used for the forward and outward movement of the Gospel into the geographical areas and spheres of human activity which are as yet out of touch with the light and truth, the healing and comfort, which the Church offers on behalf of her Lord. It is of interest in this connection to note that the East Asia Christian Conference has united the two forms of agency in its Committee for Inter-Church Aid and Mission.

Criticism and dissatisfaction with the pattern or patterns of the missionary movement have been growing in our time, particularly since the end of the Second World War. Much of this criticism is due to the fact that the pattern has not changed as rapidly as the world has changed. The end of Western domination, the rapid shift in the balance of power, the rise of the new and independent states of Asia and Africa has been so sudden and sweeping that the pattern, though it has changed in so many essentials, has not changed enough. Moreover the home constituency in our Churches does not know how much it has changed. Resentment is also fostered by the feeling in other countries that the claim to absolute truth which is made in the proclamation of Jesus Christ, the Light of the World, is somehow connected with the claim of the West to be a superior civilisation. Yet again the criticism is often directed against the structure of the Church, the deficiency of its parochial system and against institutionalism in general, on the ground that any traditional organisation, by its very rigidity, must be an obstacle to the free movement of the Spirit. Criticism of the missionary pattern can be most helpful when it proceeds from a deep concern for the establishment of a new and vital impulse of mission in all parts of the Church in all parts of the world. It is interesting to note that at the Strasbourg Conference of the World Student Christian Federation in 1960 there was a healthy reaction against globalism, against bigger international organisation, against a Geneva ideology. This was balanced by the realisation that the world Church and its mission is no more than an intellectual idea until it becomes concrete and living in terms of the congregation at the home base, wherever that may be in East or West.

Perhaps then the real thrust of the criticism is that the Church is unworthy and inadequate when confronted with the call to mission. The Church is too full of self-love, too much an introverted religious club to be able to point to Christ as the World's Redeemer. It was evident at the All-Christian Assembly for Peace, which met in Prague in June 1960, that Communists regard the Church as inherently reactionary, as an institution which is out of touch with modern life. Is that, in fact, a misunderstanding? Would not the masses of the industrial areas in Britain and the West take the same view of our present Churches? Could any of us claim that the Church's understanding of Christ as Lord has grown with the technological and scientific revolution through which we are living? In other words, is the Church from which the Christian mission proceeds living in the same world as the people to whom its mission is directed? How then can it make contact with the man in the street or in the factory, in the trade union, in the laboratory, in the senior common room? In these situations the Church is too often like a missionary in the African village or the Indian bazaar who has not yet learnt the vernacular.

The Church lacks the means of communication because its exponents do not live in the same world as those to whom it would speak.

Dr. J. H. Oldham, who was Secretary of the World Missionary Conference of 1910, was asked to write some comments on the occasion of its Jubilee in 1960. In a note published in *The Student Movement* he pointed out that the geographical expansion of the Christian faith which had been the outstanding feature of the international foreign mission of the previous hundred and fifty years had opened up into a still vaster task in the relation of the Christian faith to historical change. 'The dominant fact of our twentieth-century existence is the immeasurable and constantly accelerating increase of knowledge and the continuous transformation of human life through that knowledge.' He went on to show how this radical change meant a new problem of communication for the Church: 'In the discussion of religious beliefs it is commonly assumed that what is under discussion is a purely theological issue; that the question is whether certain beliefs are affirmed or denied. It is forgotten that these beliefs can *only* be expressed, not merely in a particular language but in a particular set of unspoken presuppositions, which we call a conceptual framework. If the basic experience of men, their ways of apprehending and feeling about the world undergo a change, then the traditional expressions of conscious beliefs must also change if they are to be understood. In the world, as it is today, there can be no future for the proclamation of the Christian message unless it is accompanied by an intellectual effort of understanding and interpretation, consciously undertaken and far surpassing in scope and difficulty the great linguistic achievements of the foreign missionary period.' [1]

[1] Article in *The Student Movement*. Summer 1960.

We cannot then speak about Christ or proclaim His Lord-ship without a clear reference to the world. To proclaim the Gospel is to speak in terms of the secular world with its many ideologies and religions, its cold war, its contrasts between the affluent society and the undernourished millions, its nationalism and colour-bar and class divisions. This is just as much the real world as the physical structure of seas and con-tinents and islands. This world which is the product of science and technology is the world to which East and West, African and European, Younger and Older Churches increasingly belong. It is the world of a civilisation which exhibits the same features in every corner of the globe. You might almost say that its presuppositions are now universal. The task of the Christian world-mission in Africa as elsewhere involves an understanding of that world. We are just beginning to realise that secularism, not Christianity, has been the missionary faith of the West. The civilisation which is based on Western science and technology has little or no room for God. Its greatest achievements are reached on the assumption that man can control nature and shape history to build a brave new world for himself and his children. It works on the principle that all parts of life can be taken separately and that life has no necessary centre, certainly not God. Moreover, the religious outlook we have inherited has largely compromised with this secular view of the meaning of human existence because it has fallen back on a secular view of religion also as one among various departments or activities of men and society, all more or less autonomous.[1]

The overwhelming dimension of the Church's missionary task is only understood when we begin to see the isolation of religion in our own society and recognise that the same

[1] Paton, W.: *The Church and the New Order*. S.C.M. Press. 1941.

danger threatens wherever the impact of this same civilisation penetrates in the non-Christian world. There are, however, two directions from which help may be expected. The first is that slowly but surely the Church is learning to understand itself as the people of God, not the church-building, not the clergy or the professionals or full-time employees of an institution and not the few who have made a speciality or hobby of something vaguely called religion. When the Church is really understood to be God's family in Christ gathered regularly for worship and instruction, but dispersed throughout the world in Africa or in Britain, at their work from Monday to Saturday, there will be less anxiety about the Church meeting the world. Then it will be apparent that the essential work of the Church is not done in church or in Christian organisations, but in the world, in trade unions, employers' associations, political parties, parent-teacher meetings; that is, in any situation where Christians and non-Christians are involved together in the same service or occupation. When in this way Christians everywhere grapple with the mission of the Church, each where he or she is engaged in a so-called 'secular' occupation, the Christian faith will take on a new relevance and urgency. The people will then look to the ministers for light on their life problems; the ministers of the Church will want more help from the teachers of the Church; and they in their turn will find that they need to listen and to learn from the laity who know the world and the problems it sets to the evangelist so much better and more responsibly than they do. Hence we may hope that the Church will find ways of training its people for the purposes of mission and service in the world and that a theology of work, a theology of the common life, will be worked out which will do for the Christian in the world what, throughout Christian history, has been done for the life of contemplation and withdrawal from the world.

For us an important aspect of this recovery and renewal of the Church as the people of God in the world is its immediate application to the members of our Churches who go overseas, and of course it applies with equal force to those who come from the lands of the Younger Churches to live and work in the West. We are beginning to see that the Christian world-mission cannot be and was not meant to be carried out by professional missionaries. In a previous section we have seen that the missionary as 'the agent of the help which one part of the Church sends to another for the discharge of the common missionary task' (p. 93), is likely to remain essential to the world-wide Church. But that in no sense lessens the vital importance and urgency of the non-professional missionary who makes his home and earns his livelihood in a country other than his own. As in the early Christian centuries, it seems that the task we have described in speaking of the Church's involvement in the world needs a multitude of non-professional Christians in business, Government service, the learned professions, industry and on the land. That, let us recall, has been the normal way by which the Gospel has spread. The missionary society and the professionally trained full-time missionary are rare phenomena in terms of Christian history. By this recovery of a truth which the early Christians knew and which companies of village folk in Africa and elsewhere still take for granted, we may greatly extend and deepen the missionary impulse which sends Christians out into the world, near at hand or far away, as messengers who bring the good tidings that Christ is on the throne of the universe.

The other direction from which we may draw encouragement is that the Younger Churches, and here we think particularly of Africa, have not yet acquired the secular attitude to life and the world which is characteristic of the West. To them the sense of the supernatural is still very close and real.

Religion for them is as naturally associated with fields and crops, with building and planting, with a town council or a political meeting as with birth or death, preaching or prayer. The question, and it is a vital one for the mission of the Church in Africa, is whether this understanding of the Gospel which belongs to a rural society living close to nature and knowing God as the God of nature as well as the God of Grace, can continue to exercise its blessings as society moves away from that simple peasant basis and divides into social classes and organisations according to means and education which belong to the stage of industrial and technical progress. When one looks closer at this question it assumes a rather startling resemblance to a still more fundamental question. We find, in fact, that we are looking at the primitive Gospel as we find it in the New Testament on the lips of our Lord Himself. His message of the Kingdom of God was given in similar terms to a people who, however their special calling and preparation set them apart from other peoples and nations, had yet this same unified outlook on life and the world. The Christian faith as it has reached us through the Old Testament, deepened and universalised by Christ through His understanding of God as Father, King and Saviour, and revealed and fulfilled in His own life and death and resurrection, is a religion of historical redemption. 'The Christian hope', as Bonhoeffer wrote, 'sends a man back to his life on earth in a wholly new way.'[1] It is not an escape from the world but a dedication to share God's purpose to change the world. To be caught up in God's work in and through Christ is to serve Him in every relation, in work or in play, in joy or in sorrow, in home or in private, in the so-called secular as in the so-called sacred. It is to discover a new kind of holy worldliness. It is to begin to

[1] *Letters and Papers from Prison.* S.C.M. Press. 1953. P. 154.

live a unified life in a divided and distraught society. The Church in Africa may yet help us in this task of proclaiming the saving Gospel of the unity of God to heal the disunity of our society. 'There are many', writes J. V. Taylor, 'who feel that the spiritual sickness of the West, which reveals itself in the divorce of the sacred from the secular, of the cerebral from the instinctive, and in the loneliness and the homelessness of individualism, may be healed through a recovery of the wisdom which Africa has not yet thrown away. The world Church awaits something new out of Africa. The Church in Buganda, and in many other parts of the continent, by obedient response to God's calling, for all its sinfulness and bewilderment, may yet become the agent through whom the Holy Spirit will teach his people everywhere how to be in Christ without ceasing to be involved in mankind, how to be bound in the bundle of life, yet at one with the Lord their God.' [1]

[1] J. V. Taylor: *The Growth of the Church in Buganda*. S.C.M. Press. 1958. P. 259 f.

SELECTED BIBLIOGRAPHY

Nuffield Foundation and Colonial Office, *African Education*. Oxford University Press. 1953.

Campbell, J. McLeod, *African History in the Making*. Edinburgh House Press. 1956.

Debrunner, H., *Witchcraft in Ghana*. Kumasi Presbyterian Book Depot. 1960.

Newbigin, Lesslie, *One Body, One Gospel, One World*. International Missionary Council. 1958.

Oliver, Roland, *The Missionary Factor in East Africa*. Longmans Green. 1952.

Parrinder, G., *Religion in an African City*. Oxford University Press. 1953.

Perham, Margery, *Lugard*. Collins. 2 vols. 1956, 1960.

Sundkler, B. J. M., *Bantu Prophets in South Africa*. Lutterworth Press. 1948.

Sundkler, Bengt, *The Christian Ministry in Africa*. Swedish Institute of Missionary Research, Uppsala. 1960.

Taylor, J. V., *Christianity and Politics in Africa*. Penguin Books. 1957.

Taylor, J. V., *The Growth of the Church in Buganda*. S.C.M. Press. 1958.

Taylor, J. V., and Dorothea Lehmann, *Christians of the Copper Belt*. S.C.M. Press. 1961.

Welbourn, F. B., *East African Rebels*. S.C.M. Press. 1961.

INDEX